MW00437669

Way Out Here in the Middle

JOHN ROACH

JONES BOOKS
Madison, Wisconsin

Copyright © 2003 John Roach
All rights reserved

Jones Books
309 N. Hillside Terrace
Madison, Wisconsin 53705-3328
www.jonesbooks.com

First edition, first printing

Photo courtesy of Mike DeVries/*The Capital Times*

All the pieces in this book were originally published in
Madison Magazine.

Library of Congress Cataloging-in-Publication Data

Roach, John.
  Way out here in the middle / John Roach.—1st ed.
    p. cm.
Columns originally published in Madison magazine.
  ISBN 0-9721217-5-7 (alk. paper)
  1. Wisconsin—Social life and customs—Anecdotes. 2. Madison
(Wis.)—Social life and customs—Anecdotes. 3. Roach, John—Anecdotes.
4. Minocqua (Wis.)—Biography—Anecdotes. 5. Country life—Wisconsin—
Minocqua—Anecdotes. 6. Minocqua (Wis.)—Social life and customs—
Anecdotes. I. Madison magazine. II. Title.
  F581.6.R63 2003
  977.4'043'092—dc22
                                                    2003020584

Printed in the United States of America

These words are dedicated to Kate, Maggie, JT and Diane Ripple Roach. Also John James Roach, and most especially to Mary Gene Heller Roach.

TABLE OF CONTENTS

TABLE OF CONTENTS

FOREWORD

On the day before I met John Roach, at a charity function where both of us were "celebrity" waiters, I was told to expect a man who was bombastic, opinionated and awfully sure of himself.

He IS bombastic, opinionated and awfully sure of himself; but that night, we became soul buddies, and he has proved to be one of the most loyal, comic, tender and talented friends and collaborators I have had the pleasure to know.

Before I ever met John, and before I read his columns, our paths had crossed unbeknownst. Those of you who didn't have the mixed blessing of growing up in Chicago may never have seen the television show called *The Sportswriters*. But all of you have seen the *Saturday Night Live* parody of the show ("Da Bulls. Da Bears...") that made John Roach, who produced that show, a legend behind the scenes. He also worked on the show that, one day seven years ago, allowed me the freedom to write stories for a living: It was then called *A.M. Chicago*. It's now called the *Oprah Winfrey Show*. When we met, he also was high on the unimagined honors heaped upon him and his great friend Mary Sweeney for their deeply quiet and lyrical screenplay, *The Straight Story*, the story of a Midwestern Diogenes who rode his lawn tractor all the way from Iowa to

Wisconsin to see his dying brother. David Lynch directed the film. Proud as punch, John remains that curious combo of humble and hopeful. It's a kick.

He also still writes a magazine column.

When I read John's columns, I occasionally disagreed, always laughed, sometimes wept, and was perennially envious because I, after all, was the columnist in this neck of the woods. However, I must cede to John in some critical respects. He writes with a man's point of view, with a pen dipped in sentiment (but never sentimentality), and he never fails to make sense—not counting on whose toes he steps. When he wrote about his advice for graduating students, and about the death of his nephew, I knew that here was a writer who was always good, but sometimes beyond compare. He examines life not with a microscope or a telescope, but with a stethoscope: Whatever John writes, he writes from the heart. John and I have the idea that one day, we two will write a movie together and spend a week on Maui with his beautiful wife Diane and my beautiful hubby Chris, toasting each other and our spouses with our collective luck and genius.

This may never happen.

This does not matter.

John Roach is an artist I am proud to call my friend, a writer I am proud to call my colleague, and the only human being with whom I would have celebrated the good results of my biopsy by dancing to Patsy Cline in the Echo Tap at three in the afternoon.

Enrich yourself. Read this book.

Jacquelyn Mitchard

INTRODUCTION

The words on the pages behind this one started at a Friday lunch at the Avenue Bar on Madison, Wisconsin's east side.

I had returned to my hometown in the mid '80s after a six year stint in Chicago, much of it in the employ of a couple of network-owned television stations where I honed my questionable skills as a producer, writer and director.

My wife Diane and I, along with our newborn daughter Kate, had made the decision to move back to Madison because every national magazine kept naming it "The Most Livable City in the Country, World and Universe." Since we were both raised here and knew this to be true, we thought it might be a good idea to bunjee down our couch, stroller and microwave and head back to the 608 area code.

The move was also motivated by the death of Diane's father and young nephew. It just seemed to us that family had become more important. As I told a Chicago friend who reacted to our announcement with shock and incredulity, "Hey Mikey, let's face it. If I was run over by a cab on the Michigan Avenue bridge, I can count on one hand the people I know here who would drive to Madison to shove my bones into the ground."

Mike thought a moment and said, "Yeah maybe. But if you were buried on a Friday you might get six, 'cause everyone likes a three day weekend.'" Shortly after we returned I met Doug Moe, another native Madisonian and the editor of *Madison Magazine*. We clicked. He had a sharp, well-read cynicism that I missed after my Chicago life and couldn't seem to glean from Madison city softball and league bowling. Doug was good enough to invite me for burgers and beer one Friday afternoon with a regular bunch at the Avenue Bar. It is there I met Jim Selk, Jeff Scott Olsen (aka Atticus), Steve Hurley and Sweet Willie Dixon among others. These guys talked smart and were.

Anyone who has ever had a beer with me knows I do one of two Irish things after the third bottle—sing or argue. On one particular afternoon I was arguing some obscure point too loudly when Doug called my bluff. "Why don't you shut up and write a column about it."

So I did. And continued to do so over the last decade and more. The columns take the form of a letter, a bit Doug and I stole from *Esquire* magazine, which is why each missive is headed by the salutation "Doug,". The later letters are addressed to Brian Howell, Doug's erstwhile successor at the magazine. It is appropriate here to thank my compatriot Matt Solomon and publisher Joan Strasbaugh for their help in compiling these notes.

I would like to claim that this compilation of columns is due to popular demand, but that would be false. Three people have suggested it. But I have always wanted to write a book and now at the age of fifty I am examining all the things I wanted to do…write a screenplay, write a book, live in an Irish castle with British servants…and realized that maybe I had already written something broadly resembling a book.

So here it is. One boomer's observations from a decade in the world's most livable city.

Written one month at a time.

Thanks. JR

THE BIG FOUR-O

Dear Doug,

Well, I bring you interesting personal news.

It comes as our generation takes over the day shift. Bill and Al, those two great southern joggers, are now large and in charge.

And just coincidentally, I turn forty this month.

I know. I know. I should be writing one of those pithy pieces about turning "THE BIG 4-0."

About my vasectomy and the way I walked for a week.

About hair growing out of my ears.

About wearing my pants either very high.

Or very low.

Asking inane Rooneyesque questions like "What is it about

men as they get older? Why do their noses begin to look like spoiled fruit. Why is that?"

But I can't bring myself to do it. I like being the age that I am.

I know it doesn't make great copy but I have three beautiful kids. A sexy wife. Business is good.

I would have to stretch to bitch.

Sure I flirt with 220. Sure I am having trouble focusing on fine print.

So my dirty little secret is that I would prefer not to drive at night.

So what?

I don't have zits.

I am not afraid of sex.

I don't live in an apartment with nine other guys.

My car starts.

I enjoy having Sunday breakfast with the woman I slept with on Saturday night.

My nose isn't bulbous. Yet.

And I bought really good firewood this year.

I am also beginning to realize a true gift of maturity.

Freedom.

Like some crusty, whittling backwoodsman, I am starting to treat dopes rudely.

I am beginning to not give a damn about petty opinions. Oh, I'm not totally oblivious to the sensitivities of others. I mean, I still bathe.

But as I approach 40, I find that I have less time to waste time.

Is that a clock I hear ticking?

I was in a meeting in Chicago last month. Pitching a project. It was a moderately high-level gathering. There were some expensive suits at the table. Some mope began telling why I would have difficulty guiding my production to fruition. After he went into his pessimistic harangue for the third time I pulled him up short and proclaimed, "Hey John. I turn 40 next month. If I wait for you to get enthused about a project, I'll be dead. This will happen. With or without you."

The other guys at the table pricked up their ears. The thing is happening.

It was kinda fun being up on my hind legs.

This isn't happening all of a sudden, however.

It is melodrama to assume that the curtain of middle age drops abruptly as you take the call at 40.

The onset of middle age seems to come in fits and bursts.

Your little sister gets gray hair.

Your son races you down the driveway. You work to keep it close.

Your nine-year-old daughter turns her head and laughs. For a moment she looks like a woman.

Middle age began for me in Boston.

I was thirty-seven.

I was shooting Dennis Miller at The Garden. You got it. The Hallowed Parquet. At lunch a game ensued.

We were going two-on-two. Our opponents were two younger stagehands. Strong, but a lot of wasted motion. Poor passers. They had never seen anyone fight through a pick in their lives.

My shot had nice rotation that day and was dropping enough to engender heckling from the crew.

With three seconds of my youth remaining, I put up an 18 foot jump shot from just inside and left of the key.

With two seconds left in my prolonged boyhood the shot caromed off the iron and came deep to the left comer.

I moved to the ball.

In the last second in the life of Young John, I picked the ball off the second bounce and planted my left foot to turn and shoot again.

A sharp bang.

I still can't believe the soft tissue around the knee called the anterior cruciate and medial collateral ligaments can make that much noise.

But they did.

I fell to the parquet (nice touch, eh?). Thought I might toss breakfast for a moment. Went a little cold and shocky. I remember thinking at that moment that I had become old.

Eventually finished the shot. Returned to Madison via Northwest and wheel chair.

The pain didn't interfere with my sleep that night but I kept jerking awake. I kept hearing my knee explode.

It was yelling good-bye to the days when I could do anything I wanted.

The next morning I asked the good doctor for the prognosis.

"Well, John, if you were a young athlete I would operate on you today," he said.

"Doc. I *am* a young athlete," I replied.

He laughed.

What the hell. You can't run without a limp forever. Besides, I take more pleasure watching my son run than running myself. Certainly worth the price of bidding one's knee adieu. Such is the trade.

But there is the downside of 40. It has to do with all those good-byes.

Wife Diane ran into Susan at Hilldale the other day. She gave Di a big hug. My wife was a bit surprised by this as she had just seen her at volleyball the week before. Diane asked her how she was doing. "Not so well," Susan replied. "I was just diagnosed with breast cancer. I start chemo next week."

"Say good-bye to my hair," she said.

There are even tougher good-byes.

A man died last month. He influenced my life. He was healthy. And then he died in his sleep.

The last time I talked with George he was telling us to let ourselves into his new cabin in Manitowish Waters. We could wait and chat when he got back from dinner with friends.

We stopped by the empty retreat. We idled in the quiet. The smell of new knotty pine. A lone loon calling on the lake. It was drizzling and twilight.

The kids were getting tired so we left. I didn't cry for George till I got to his funeral. I leafed through the program. Then Diane, eyes misting, pointed to the cover. It was a hand-drawn picture of the cabin.

We had been thinking about building our own place some day up North. When we got older.

We break ground this month.

Regards,
John

February 1993

HOME ALONE 3

Dear Doug,

She left.
Packed her bags.
Walked out the door.
Now it's just me, Kate, Maggie and Johnny.
And a note about medications and car pools.

Lest you start fixing me up with a friendly trollop or someone's cousin, you should know that Diane will return Sunday night. She merely escaped on a Virgin Islands getaway with her sisters.

They are married with children so they cannot technically lay claim to the Island's moniker.

But enough of that, let me tell you about my week.

Call it *Home Alone 3: Mom's Gone*.

My wife's junket began three months before she ever left. No benign escape from the husband and the kids can be truly enjoyed without a good twelve weeks of worry preceding departure.

Diane worried about the flight, tropical insects, unrest in the Islands, the food, tropical insects, exchange rates, the weather, the drinking water and tropical insects.

T-minus thirty days marked the beginning of the phone calls. It is S.O.P. for all Catholic sisters going anywhere to phone each other every five minutes until departure.

They must confirm their mutual anxiety.

It is a living thing.

The West Side telephone exchanges were critically overworked. There was a rumor afoot that the entire family would be given an 800 number.

Departure day coincided with all three of the kids getting sick. Maternal guilt lay heavy on the land. So did the wads of Kleenex. It did not seem to matter that the kids were all inflicted with your garden variety grade school colds.

The same ones they have had since September, 1987.

This prompted the last minute "I can't go" reflex. I talked her down.

Diane was still debating as she stuffed her bags in the trunk. She had packed three swimming suits, drinking water, a jar of peanut butter and four loaves of banana bread.

No lie.

She distributed hugs and kisses. Whispered tender words of

thanks in my ear. And then she was off. The children and I waved farewell. We missed her already.

She was back in three minutes.

She had forgotten the slip of paper with her confirmation numbers. She found it under the Christmas decorations. Then she was really off.

And now for my week.

Sunday.

Discover kids don't like watching CNN.

Rented *Fern Gully*, *Troop Beverly Hills* and *The Great Outdoors*. Kids fight for seven hours over which one to watch. Eventually they all climb on my lap to watch the Cable News Network.

In a fit of activity we go grocery shopping. I buy food for a family of seventy. I make chili for dinner.

They want Cocoa Puffs.

Johnny wants to play War or Slap. These are card games that he has just learned. He asks me every three minutes to play one of these games.

Kate has me look at her sore throat every half hour.

Maggie won't leave my side.

In a strange way, I like the activity. It's a different family dynamic with Mom absent. I am no longer chopped liver. I am the main act.

This would be interesting for maybe one more day.

At 7 p.m. I get a call from an important client. Needs me to fly to New York Monday a.m. Big stuff. I take a deep breath and explain to this man, to whom I never say no, that I cannot go. I tell him why.

A slight pause and he says, "Hey John, let's cover it some other way. Family always comes first."

I won't forget.

Diane calls. She has arrived safely. She's worrying about the kids medication. If the amoxicillin isn't working I am to call and get them another miracle drug.

The weather is perfect.

They can buy rum for two dollars a bottle.

Meanwhile, back in the Roach household it is bedtime. They all want to sleep with me, exhibiting the first signs of MAW...Maternal Affection Withdrawal.

After much negotiating, and many drinks of water, they sleep. In my bed.

I drink a beer.

Day One has ended. Seven more to go.

And I wonder if I have enough life insurance on Diane.

Monday.

Day Two.

My sister Sue arrives. She is handling daytime duties while I'm at work. She is a godsend.

Quick business trip down the road. I call home twice in the morning to check on the kids. What a dad.

Ring into the office after the show. One message leaps out at me. "Call home!"

I hang up and hit the programmed number on the car phone.

Did Johnny fall? Does Maggie need stitches? Has Kate's fever spiked dangerously?

Sister Sue picks up.

"Hi. Everything's fine. Just wanted you to tell me how to use the Stairmaster in the basement."

I exhale.

This night we have a family talk about missing mom.

Kate is nine, and although she will not cop to actually missing her mother she has had a string of mysterious maladies. Sore throat. Headache. Leg pain. I ask her what she misses most about her

Mom. She just shrugs and smiles a bit sadly.

Maggie is six. She is Diane's shadow. With a pout on her face she proclaims that she misses Mom's "hugs and kisses."

Johnny, the youngest at five, states in true Oedipal fashion that he misses not only the hugs and kisses but "Mom's whole body."

Can't argue with that.

Day Three.

I walk to the door. The kids are all over me.

They have gone into Affection Debt. The big fight tonight is about who gets to sit on what part of my lap.

Just as they are settled, Kate remembers that *Full House* starts at seven. All three dash upstairs to watch it on the small set in our bedroom. Eventually they go to sleep. In my bed. Again.

I go upstairs at ten. I awaken Kate and she sleepwalks to her bed. I lift Maggie and carry her to the bottom bunk. Johnny's cough has been bad so I leave him lie.

I never drink beer at home when Diane's around but downstairs watching the news I crack one.

Well, Doug, I'll catch you later.

Johnny just did the Big Spit on my bed sheets.

It smells like Cocoa Puffs.

Regards,
John

March 1993

AMONG THE BUILDING IMPAIRED

Dear Doug,

1-90/94 to 78 through Westfield, Wautoma and Coloma. Beyond the "Tension Line" to Stevens Point and Wausau. Onward…there goes Merrill. An Indian campfire mural adorns the barn of some enlightened farmer who obviously is not apoplectic about spearing.

I am onto the two-lane now. Tomahawk whizzes by. There's a dead deer. Hazelhurst cannot be far off and then it's a clear shot on the four-lane into Minocqua. From there I'm only a few minutes from our joint in the woods.

Our lodge on the lake.

Remember that cabin I told you about while I was in the throes of my 40th?

Well, we built it.

I am, however, taking tremendous liberty with the plural pronoun "we." Fact is, I've driven nary a nail. Haven't pushed a circular saw. Ain't hauled any lumber. The only callus I have is from writing checks.

At this happiest of moments, when I have realized my Waldenesque dream. I am battling another emotion.

Embarrassment.

You see. Doug, when it comes to the manly tools and acts of construction, I am the guy they pick last.

I handle tools the way Mary Murphy handles young athletes. Poorly.

This cabin, which will one day be liberating, is, in the short term, emasculating

First there was Scott, the general contractor. He helped us buy the land. The bulk of our discussions centered around the building site's ability to hold a septic system. My mind was abuzz with terms like "perc test," "Class One soil" and "gravity flow."

I couldn't understand why I was being forced to spend weeks contemplating the processing of yesterday's meal when all I wanted to discuss was the view.

Then Scott produced the plans. I bluffed my way through much of this stage. I would puff up my chest, point to the blueprints and ask, "What is this?"

"That's a door," Scott would reply, suppressing the urge to roll his eyes.

"Very good," I would say. "I like doors. Carry on."

My charade dissolved when the actual construction began. That's when Jerry and the boys arrived.

Jerry is the construction foreman. He actually knows the names of tools. He uses tools all the time. These actions threaten my manhood.

Jerry is a NASCAR-driving, deer-hunting, walleye-catching, rip-sawing, wood-staining, tool-belt, table-saw kind of guy.

He uses words like "plumb," "soffit" and "headers."

Guys like Jerry are the ones who will survive a nuclear exchange. On the morning after Armageddon they will build a home, shoot a meal and then go shopping for a trolling motor that same evening.

I have an image of me at Jerry's back door, cowering in the radioactive ash, begging for fish guts to feed my family.

Jerry calls me "The Yuppie." Then he chuckles.

There is another thing about these construction guys that troubles me. Women like them. Maybe it's the sweat. Maybe it's the fact that they can actually fix things around the house. Or maybe women simply like the fact that most of these guys have jean-clad posteriors smaller than their husband's chins.

Yes, I think that might be it.

My relationship with Jerry is not so much class struggle as culture clash. I told Jerry that my wife and I had been arguing about the cabinets. Jerry told me the last time he argued with his wife was when she forgot to send in his application to bow-hunt bear.

I never mentioned the cabinets again.

Much of my insecurity with this tool stuff stems from my upbringing. I grew up in a home where every doorknob came off in your hand.

My dad had one tool and he didn't know its name.

I remember one incident in particular. The Roach men were trying to move a queen-sized mattress to our third floor attic. It would not fit through the door. Dad took our only tool (I think it's called a hammer), and pounded at the doorway until it was larger. The door remained in that battered condition, leaking plaster, splinters and dust for another decade. Then my folks moved to a condo.

The men in our family were not wimps. My father was an athlete, as were my brothers and myself. But what good is a jump shot when the eaves are leaking?

My father's aptitude for tools runs in my blood. One spring, flush with the pride of a young father, I took it upon myself to assemble a swing set for the kids.

Bad idea.

The instructions claimed that the damn thing could be "easily assembled."

What it did not say was that you needed 45 thousand bucks worth of tools to do it.

They maintain F-16's with fewer tools than it took to put this swing together.

Fifteen minutes into the project I was swearing, weeping in frustration, throwing tools and pounding my bead with my fists. Diane grabbed the children and ran to the basement.

The kids thought this had something to do with a tornado.

The next day Diane had a handyman come over to correctly construct the thing.

"I just want to make sure the kids are safe," she explained with pity in her voice.

I stayed in my room with the shades drawn.

And that is why this cabin thing has embarrassed me. Because Jerry and his Guys can do things that I can't. They do them in a cavalier way that I envy.

They act like everyone knows how to install a toilet.

I truly wish I could build and fix things. Actually create stuff out of wood and stone and nails. Things that people would touch and appreciate. The grain of the wood. The hang of a door.

Things that would be standing after I am dead.

But that is not to be. Jerry jokes that they'll let me pound one nail on my cabin, and they'll have a photographer and the paramedics standing by.

Ah well.

I had one brief moment of consolation in the midst of this assault on my manhood. I told Jerry I was going to write about the cabin. I asked if he wanted to help.

Jerry's face grew pale. His knees began to shake. Fear turned his eyes the color of drywall.

And then he invited me fishing.

Regards,
John

June 1993

AGING GRACEFULLY

Dear Doug,

I don't know why, but lately I've been having a hard time with older folks.

It is Mother's Day.

My gift to Diane is to pick up her 96-year-old grandmother at the nursing home and deliver her to the in-laws' Momfest. This is not pleasurable.

The car pulls into the circular drive. The lot is full. Ma Day means big business at the home.

A harried receptionist directs me to Granny's room. It is all the way down the hall.

I run a gauntlet of lives.

One room is a cluttered shrine to the Blessed Virgin.

The next is totally spartan, no signs of human occupancy except for the very old man sitting motionless in his wheel chair centered in the room. The window is open to the breeze, but the curtains do not move. All is utterly, totally, still.

The next room is loud. A throbbing contemporary bass track. An ancient woman has her head four inches from the TV screen. At first I think she is watching MTV and I am amused. But then I see that it is *Star Search*.

Does this stir memories for her? *Ted Mack's Original Amateur Hour*. There are no new ideas.

As I turn a toothless woman with small, wild eyes clutches at

14

me from her wheelchair. She yells in gibberish. Startled. I move past her. She continues to grab at the spot where I was.

My discomfort is total. I arrive at Granny's room.

She fails to recognize me. Finally, with the help of an attendant we make it to the car. She remembers my name as we pull onto the Beltline.

If I am lucky I will live to be this way. Some luck.

Later in the day I mention this episode to my own mother. She remarks "I hate that place. Don't put me there."

I laugh and wish her Happy Mother's Day. She is in her early sixties. She is not smiling.

The next day in the office, Dr. Kevorkian is staring at me from the cover of *Time* as I open another angry letter from a business associate who is now past seventy. The tone, as usual, is insulting. He has no use for any generation other than his own. Nor does he cotton to fax machines, Fed Ex, car phones and computers.

I wish he was avuncular, benign and wise. He isn't.

It would be best if he acknowledged that his generation's torch is being passed. He won't. If anyone gets a torch from this guy they are going to have to knock him on his ass and grab it. Problem is, he can't carry the thing anymore. Blinded by ego and fear, he refuses to see this.

I want to spare myself a similar fate. Learn from the wise elders on how to age well. Take some mental notes.

One learns first from one's parents. I've been watching John and Mary Gene as they approach seniordom.

Mom is not a senior (this qualifier guarantees me food and babysitting for the next year), but all the kids are gone.

She is getting in shape to be old. She plays scrabble 80 times a week with a heady bunch of tile freaks who use words only people who play Scrabble use. Flkarburang. Gondltry. Eog.

When she isn't playing Scrabble she studies with her French

group. She has been studying French for the last decade. They sit, eat croissants, and talk Francoise. I suspect these people are in her Scrabble group.

French Scrabble cannot be far off.

She also plays a lot of bridge. In English.

She complains about her back and my Dad.

She is afraid that her final years will be spent in a nursing home. Her youth included a lengthy stay at an orphanage. She is understandably institution-phobic. A tough way to bookend a life.

There is fear in my mother's voice when she discusses these things.

Aging lessons I've learned from Mom…Stay active. Work the brain. Do the things you never had time to do with the kids, or spouse, hanging on your waist. Even if you have a sore back, act young. Don't make up fake Scrabble words. Confront your fears.

The observations on Dad…Pa is less socially active than Mom. Ergo her complaints about him.

My Dad's years of work-related travel have turned him into a bit of a homebody. His day includes reading the paper for two hours and then watching the Cubs. As a road-weary traveler myself I find this lifestyle appealing,

Dad has changed with his retirement. He is more relaxed. He's great with the grandkids. He'll come over and watch them, claiming, "Call anytime. Hell, I've got nothing to do. I'm retired." He'll chuckle.

Now that he no longer works, he laughs more.

He seems less fearful of old age and death than Mom. He's even bought his cemetery plot and tombstone. The stone is engraved. Only the date of his demise needs chiseling.

When Mom suggests that his preparations are macabre he responds, "What the hell…we're all going to die!"

To which Mom responds, "Yes, I know. But you're not supposed to be organized about it!"

If Dad has a fault of old age it is that he repeats himself. Maybe it's genetic.

Maybe it's genetic.

Lessons learned from Dad...Don't be afraid to give up the reins a little. Get on the floor with the grandkids. Find something to do with the wife. Watch lots of baseball.

Here are some more notes. I'll pull them out when I hit 65....

I will not drone on about the past. If someone wants a history lesson, I'll let them ask.

I'll dress dapper. Comb my hair. Bathe. To feel young it is good to look young. Wearing clothes without cigarette burns has that effect.

On the other hand, I will not subject myself to disfiguring plastic surgery. Some of these subjects look like all their old skin is tied up in a bun under their hat.

When I am old I will remember to smile. Wrinkles make you look mean unless you grin. Upon smiling, however, wrinkles become an asset, making all old people look like Wilford Brimley or Jessica Tandy.

If they have their teeth in.

I will work to pay kind attention to children without smothering or scaring them. I will always have candy for them the way my grandmother did for me. As my father does for my kids. Screw the dentist.

I will not fear or ridicule change. If there is dumb change, I will smile and shake my head. When my grandchildren ask me why, I will try to state my position with wisdom, and in doing so, teach.

A final note. It comes after a business dinner to which I had been invited as a guest.

The evening's proceedings included a toast and award to a senior associate.

He was forced, due to illness, to retire at an age earlier than expected.

He rose to say good-bye to his coworkers. Good-bye to the power and status that had defined him in his working life.

He walked slowly to the rostrum as his friends rose to salute him. Then, eyes misting, he said simply, "Thank you for allowing me to retire with dignity."

He turned and walked back to his seat.

Dignity.

Got to remember that one.

Regards,
John

July 1993

A DEATH AT DUSK

Dear Doug,

The thunderstorms have rumbled off to the east. Funnel clouds were eyed near town. Now they're bothering Walworth County.

A beautiful sunset remains. I leave the clamor of the house to take a stroll. Walk off the red meat and potato. The air is left clean and cool in the storm's wake.

Hardly seems the time to watch a young man die.

As I near the corner, the crackle of police radio dialogue rides by in the breeze. Turning, the flashing lights come into view. Many of them. I turn to walk across the park toward the scene.

I come up a rise. A young family is silhouetted in the red gleam of burning flares. I am puzzled. There are four flames behind them, creating a brilliant square in the parking lot by the pool. My first thought is that there has been a drowning. A child left unattended.

Lost in the loud screams and cannonball dives.

But then I see the scene. Emergency vehicles of every type
are alongside the road up the street. As I move closer I see the
crowd. Their heads are turning, looking upward. Low and slow on
the horizon I see it now. The Trauma Chopper. The flares are a
landing zone.

It settles to the earth, the wind and noise so disturbing.

I turn my head from the blades' gale. My eye falls on the car. It
is molded around a large walnut tree. Tree One. Car Zero.

The windshield is gone. A team of firemen, policemen and
paramedics are huddled around the front seat. One worker is
standing on the hood. Someone in the group near me mumbles
"the jaws of life."

The onlookers are a mixed lot. Witnesses. Kids. Teenagers.

Three old Irish farmers in overalls. They have come to gawk.
Pray. Hope. We are all keenly aware that another member of the
species is fighting for his life 30 yards away.

We do not know him, but he is our brother. Our son.

And the tribe looks on.

The whispers and huddles bring out the story. Two kids racing.
Lost control. Almost hit two women head-on in the oncoming
lane.

"That was us!" a stout young woman says from the fringe of our
group, "If we'd had another coat of paint on the car he woulda hit
us. It was that close." She looks to her girlfriend for corroboration.
Pale, she nods.

More than a few in the bunch comment on the drivers who
barrel down this old farm road just outside the Madison city limits.
"They should leave this car here for a year. Make kids look at it,"
an old-timer grumbles.

A guy my age turns to me, "When I think of what I did as a
kid. I'm lucky to be alive." Ditto.

"Kid in the squad was his friend. Was drivin' the car he was racin'," someone else remarks out the side of his mouth.

I see the friend in the back seat of the cop car. His baseball hat is pulled down low. His face is ashen. Skin taut. He stares at the scene. At his buddy. The flashing lights catch his face. He will live this night forever.

And I wonder how this will change him.

I speak quietly to a civilian who is waving a flashlight in the street. Turns out he and his wife saw it from the house. They got to the car pretty quick. The woman's eyes are slightly wild as she says, "They've called the parents, but they're not home." This bothers her. Her husband is more composed. His eyes are simply sad. They both saw him up close. Neither of them will sleep early tonight.

They have lifted him out of the car to the sound of the chopper winding down. They lay the stretcher on the road.

Two doctors are on the scene. They arrived in the bird. The bald one is in red jogging pants and a T-shirt. He works very quickly around the perimeter of the action. The younger one, in blue scrubs, is immediately lost in the scrum of attendants that surround the body.

Every once in a while you can catch a glimpse of the young man. He is wearing a cervical collar. They are bagging him, breathing for him. They are taking turns pumping on his chest.

His hair is brown.

Everyone is hurrying. A fireman brings an extra bottle of oxygen. An IV is opened. Another fireman holds the bag of fluid over the boy. The doctor in the jogging pants turns to one kit after another. Now everyone is putting on surgical gloves. More large packages are opened, their wrappings thrown hurriedly to the ground. More dashes back to the ambulance. The rhythmic chest pumping continues, with different personnel, like some macabre relay.

The faces of the workers are grim. Their gazes do not acknowledge the onlookers. The import of their actions deny them that luxury.

And the sun has set. The many lights have now created the most awful of stages. The great limbs of the walnut tree look down on it all from the balcony.

It has been nearly an hour since the accident, but the crowd does not leave. Activity is hope.

But then, out of the middle emerges the young doctor in the scrubs. He stands, his head down. He strips off his gloves. The circle loosens. Activity subsides. A paramedic removes the breathing apparatus. Through the foreground a policeman begins to walk past the body with a measuring wheel, chronicling the length of the skid. He has business to do. The reality of what has happened washes over the crowd. There is a collective sigh and groan. The young married couple in front of me quietly hug each other. One of the old farmers next to me mutters, "Damn shame." His eyes are damp.

Two firemen bring out a white sheet and, with a quiet air of respect, create a curtain around the body. The balding doctor opens a yellow plastic sheet. It disappears behind the white drape. The emergency crew drifts away. Only one gives the predictable shake of the head towards the crowd. The others are lost in their thoughts or jobs.

Three firemen place the blood-soaked instruments and bandages in red Hazardous Waste bags. Now there are only two firemen by the body. Yet they still hold the sheet.

The coroner, in sports coat and Elvis hair, arrives. He is cavalier. Seems to like the lights. Still, a tough job.

The two doctors, heads down, make their way back to the Sky Beast. Its rotors slap the air. It lifts and moves away. Its lights become the stars in the western sky, reflecting down on the boy left behind.

Only the two firemen on curtain duty stand watch now. All

others have assumed other tasks. Fire trucks and ambulances are backed away. The crowd dwindles. Neighbors walk home arm in arm.

I make my way home through the darkness of the park. A breeze, a ghost, runs through the black trees. Chilled, I say a quiet prayer for a name I'll read in the morning paper.

I turn for one last look at the scene from afar. I see the two firemen set the white sheet over the young man in the road. They walk away.

He is alone now.

He is free.

Regards,
John

September 1993

1994

THE SUN ALSO RISES

Dear Doug,

The winter has been long. The raw cold of January. The snows of February. The winter storm warnings that continue to be posted through late March into early April.

Winters are a struggle, and none so much as this one. The ice on our lake up north is over two feet thick. I have been wearing a winter coat all my life.

The news doesn't help. Television adds only the color of blood to liven up the final gray days of the cold season.

CNN is a depressing drone.

There is a litany of tawdry news that would matter less if we were not housebound by ice and snow. The Bobbitts. Tonya and Nancy. Michael and his little boys. The Menendez brothers. The Quake and its aftershocks.

Citizens going to market to buy bread become mortar fodder in the old Yugoslavia. Israelis and Palestinians find new and more manic ways to kill each other. In Washington, instead of handling the people's business, Bill and Hillary are dogged by a two-bit Arkansas land deal.

And in Madison, Mayor Paul returns home from emergency cardiac surgery. While his heart should be resting, it is forced to beat fast as he and his wife bundle up their children and run them out into the dark, cold street when some cretin tries to torch his home.

A cholesterol and arson victim all in one week. Tough winter.

I ran out of firewood in early February, just in time for the big snows. Instead of enjoying a crackling fire and a good book, I ate bad, fatty food and wore down the batteries of the remote control. Winter has made me fat, stupid, sallow and dull.

But worse than that, it has made me sour with despair. Haunting business problems have jerked me awake at 3 a.m. Just me, one light, and the chime of a clock. At that time of night, at this time of year, there seems no escape.

No hope.

But then it happens. First there was Dan Jansen's Last Ride. If anyone had a right to wallow in despair, it would have been that falling Milwaukee boy. But he persevered against doubt and history.

Then, a week later, walking out to get the morning paper at 6 a.m., I heard them high overhead. Geese, northbound.

And then I was invited to The Party.

It was to be another gathering of my wife's family. A Pizza Party in late March. Billed as "Say Good-Bye to Winter." A bonfire. A special surprise guest. Big deal.

These are events that I try to avoid. Too many screaming children. Too many Big Catholic Family conversations that aren't conversations at all, just words shouted through the bedlam.

The festivities were to be held at Tom and Sue's. Tom is Diane's older and only brother. Sue is his lovely wife. Party aside, they are two of the more remarkable people I have ever met.

Death has made them that way.

Tom and Sue had two sons. Jeff, the oldest, is a junior at Michigan. On July 26, 1984, their youngest boy, seven-year-old Andy, was riding his bike on the sidewalk with a gaggle of neighborhood boys along a quiet tree-lined street on the west side. They were following the garbage truck as it made its weekly route.

The details are hard to write. Andy crossed at the corner hoping to follow the truck on its usual path up the street. But the truck turned into him. The driver did not see the Boy, the Son, the Brother, the Grandson, the Nephew, the Cousin, the Friend.

Andy was run over and killed instantly.

Someone ran to get Sue. She collapsed on the front lawn. They wouldn't let her near her son's body.

Tom was called at work. His car screeched to a halt at the scene, the driver's door left open as he rushed out to meet the worst moment of his life.

They buried Andy two days later.

A haunting incident occurred after the funeral, during the reception held in the family's back yard. I was talking with Tom. He was shaken but strong on that saddest summer afternoon. Suddenly our words were drowned out by a low-flying squadron of jets. As the four fighters flew overhead, one peeled away in the Missing Man Formation.

Tom had a friend who was an Air National Guard pilot. A friend who knew Andy loved jets.

I still hear Tom's deep, long sigh as he looked up into the sky.

For many months after the death of their son, Tom and Sue bore that haunted, awful look of grieving parents. They both dropped weight. Tom, a regular churchgoer, stopped going altogether.

But slowly they rebounded. Unable to have any more children, they became the second parents to a whole wave of nieces and nephews. When any of us needed a toddler break or a quick vacation without the kids (usually to conceive more of them), Tom and Sue were there. With the possible exception of Pizza Hut or Jumping Jack's, Tom and Sue's home is still our kids' favorite destination.

So it was with enthusiasm that Diane and the brood headed out to their place for the Pizza Party, Mystery Guest and bonfire.

I grudgingly decided to attend at the last moment, when an NCAA tournament game I was watching didn't go into overtime.

The pizzas arrived. But just before the feeding frenzy began, Sue asked everyone, all 40 sisters, in-laws, nieces and nephews and grandparents that make up this big family, to hold hands and offer a prayer.

Cynic that I am, I did not hold anyone's hand. I'll pray over turkey or ham, but I could not bring myself to pray over pizza.

After grace, Tom spoke up.

In a clumsy little speech, he explained that the much-awaited Mystery Guest wouldn't be arriving until late August. He continued to explain, with a glowing smile, as a blushing Sue lifted her oversized sweater to reveal a belly swollen with four and a half months of child. That they were going to name the new arrival "Goober" or "Thelma Lou."

In their mid 40s, a full 17 years after the birth of their last child and 10 years after his death, Tom and Sue were going to be a Mom and Dad once more.

After the tears, bedlam and cries of incredulity from the gathered clan, I asked Tom how son Jeff, now 20 years old, took the news.

"Not too well," Tom said.

"Yeah," I responded. "I am sure it brings back some tough memories for him of Andy."

"No, that's not it," Tom joked. "I think he just couldn't deal with the fact that his parents were still having sex."

Tom, not one for complicated philosophy, also remarked, "More than anything, it makes me think about the randomness of life. Andy was taken from us so quickly, and now this new little life surprises us. You want to plot out your whole life, but you really don't have as much control of things as you think. You just gotta have hope."

So there you have it.

The snow is vanishing. Dan Jansen is a millionaire. And Tom and Sue are going to be chaperoning prom when they are sixty.

And you know, Doug. I think this just might be the year the Cubs win the pennant.

Ain't spring grand?

Regards,
John

May 1994

FUTURE SHOCK

Dear Doug,

I stumble upon the picture occasionally. The kid wearing the blue graduation cap and gown, flanked by the beaming parents. Behind them, the white house. The peonies are in bloom.

It is a photographic remnant of America's springtime rite of passage. A memory of the day I cast off the shackles of high school.

More than 20 years have passed since that day, but I still feel a rush of emotion when the latest crop of kids breeze by in their flowing gowns, giddy and buzzed with all the promise that Graduation Day holds.

But when I see these young people, Doug, I am also angered.

I am irate because I have never been asked to do what so many loud, over-opinionated people like myself long to do.

I have never been asked to give a commencement address.

But if I were asked, it would go something like this:

Ahem. Thank you for that wonderful introduction, Superintendent Wilhoyte.

By the way, it's *John* Roach. Jim Roach is my brother. And Cheryl...nice hair.

Let me begin with the words of musician and poet Paul Simon..."When I look back on all that crap I learned in high school, it's a wonder I can think at all."

Please bear in mind that the guy who wrote those words now wears an incredibly bad toupee.

And that is my first piece of advice for you young men and women who are preparing to walk that long and winding road, riding that boat of knowledge out onto the eternity of the future with the waves of forever washing over your amber waves of grain. No matter how bald you become, or how bad your perm is, DON'T WEAR FAKE HAIR. You will never fool smart people, and they are the very folks you have to bluff in order to succeed on this long trip we call "Life."

Dumb clucks are easy to fool, but they usually don't have anything you want.

And, another thing. Take a good look around at the people in your class. Gawk at each other's bodies for a minute or two. Hell, it's not like you haven't been doing it since middle school. Now memorize what you've just seen, because never again will your stomachs be so flat, your breasts so firm, your cheeks so taut, your eyes so unlined. Bodywise, it's all downhill from here.

In fact, here's a cool trick. If you really want to figure out how your friends are going to look at your 25th High School Reunion, turn around and look at the parents in the bleachers. Now, find your parents.

That is you in the year 2019.

Hey, reality bites.

And, for your edification, assuming you know what that words means, here is a quick guide to your upcoming high school reunions.

The Fifth—Don't go. Nothing has really changed. You will not have a good time with your classmates who do attend, because they actually miss high school. Scary.

The Tenth—Go. You will be amazed at how many of your classmates are already married. And divorced. Guys, you will notice women in your class whom you ignored for four years. They have now blossomed into remarkably attractive, worldly, confident creatures. They will have three drinks and remind you that you treated them like toxic waste. They will then introduce you to their Chicago boyfriends who make more money than you and let you know it.

The Fifteenth—Don't go. Nothing much has really changed from the tenth and the only folks there will be the ones from the fifth.

The Twentieth—Be sure to go. Middle age is now rearing its ugly head. This is the reunion where someone walked up to me and said, "Wow, whoever thought you would get fat?" This is also the reunion where people have finally cast off the haunting remains of their high school personas. Everyone has forgotten each other's dopey high school nicknames and the embarrassing details of exactly who did what with whom at prom. In fact, you almost have fun.

The Twenty-fifth—Go. You don't have that many years left.

One final high school reunion tip. If you are married, never dance more than twice with your old high school flame. Strange things happen when the old music is playing.

No one likes a long speech, so here are a few quick notes to help all of you with life after graduation.

Move out of your house tomorrow. Adult kids and parents were never meant to live in the same building. And you are now an adult. Deal with it.

Go away to school. You can reinvent yourself. There are few opportunities in life to get such a clean break from your past. And a lot of you need it.

And here is something I had to learn the hard way when I moved out: When doing laundry, remember to sort. Whites, darks, and lights.

More notes. Never use hard alcohol to actually quench your thirst. If you start with beer, stay with beer. If someone suggests doing a shot, take it, pour it casually on the floor when no one is looking. Then slam the shot glass on the bar and proclaim, "That was great. Let's do another one." Repeat. Then drive for the idiot.

Remember, nothing good happens after midnight. Interesting, yes. Good, no.

A few more notes. I'm almost finished.

You are better off buying one good shirt than two cheap shirts.

Don't be in a hurry to decide on a career. Too many people who knew what they wanted to do when they were 18 are miserable at 40.

Be careful driving at dusk in the country. You might hit a deer.

Don't get married until you are 26 or older.

Hit on 16. Stay on 17.

Don't trust people who say, "Trust me."

For married men, cleaning the kitchen without being asked is the best foreplay.

Don't whine. If you are unhappy, do something about it or shut up.

Stay away from people who have lengthy, detailed conversations with their pets. Especially if the animal is wearing a sweater.

Learn how to drive in America. Stay the hell out of the passing lane unless you are going eighty or faster.

Never let anyone sign checks for you.

Have kids. Hug them a lot. It will pay off later.

Don't rush your backswing.

Call out the pick.

Always have a book going. It is the fundamental low-tech experience other than sex. And buy hard covers. It heightens the experience.

Never, ever wear real tight pants after the age of 28.

And, finally, in closing, remember this: You have value to us all, what you do makes a difference. You have an obligation to achieve. That's part of the deal when you chose to become a human.

Oh. One more thing. Almost forgot.

If you really want to catch fish, use live bait.

Regards,
John

June 1994

THE HIGH ROAD

Dear Doug,

In honor of your "Best of Madison" edition, I've got a story for you.

I first heard about it from my neighbor. He and I share a common concern. I've written about it before. It has to do with the treatment of children. And the actions of adults.

Wait 'til you hear what happened. You'll love it. And you'll wonder why no one has done this before.

It all started at Warner Park and Lakeview School on the first weekend of June. Scads of parents, kids and coaches gathered there for the annual Madison Area Youth Soccer Association tournament. Children six and older getting together to kick the ball around and score the occasional goal.

Madison's prepubescent answer to the World Cup.

For the most part, the whole thing looked like a soft drink commercial. Cottonwood fluff floated in the air. The early summer sun warmed the proud parents and grandfolks lining the field in lawn chairs, with many of the fans shouting encouragement to the colorful dots scampering across the field—their kids.

Unfortunately, not all of the adults were benign.

Too many were screaming instructions and commands in varying crescendos, about a game they had never played, to young ones who were innocently struggling to learn about the simplest concepts of teamwork, competition, sweat and soccer.

Some of the large humans were simply ignorant.

Some were neurotic.

The worst were abusive.

I guess the word "abuse" is overused these days.

Let's just call them jerks.

I saw one full-grown, corpulent male stand alone behind a goalie—a 10-year-old girl and attempt to intentionally distract her by talking and yelling at her. An official finally had to stop the game and instruct this alleged adult to move away.

If the guy had been wearing a trench coat, he would have been arrested.

But these things happen. I try to sit back and let the coaches handle the game. When the adult bellowing becomes deafening, however, I occasionally bark out: "Don't listen to any of this!" This garners a scowl from my wife as I embarrass her.

But this was rare. And our kids were lucky to have good coaches.

Good teachers.

Some of the young competitors at this tournament, though, were not so lucky. And therein lies the story.

It was a game played by the Verona Vipers. A Friday evening contest against a team from McFarland.

The Vipers were actually a bit too innocent to live up to their fearsome nickname.

They were just children.

Third graders. Eight and nine year olds.

The team—13 boys and two girls—was pretty good. They won eight games during the regular season while losing two. The tournament would be a fun and exciting end to the season.

But it was not to be.

Jon Spencer is an assistant coach for the Verona Vipers. His son plays on the team. Jon is a teacher. Coaches at Memorial. Early on in the game he began to have a problem with the other coach. The guy was complaining a lot to the official.

And please let the record show—the official was 12 years old. The soccer association has some of the older kids call the youngsters' games.

When the McFarland coach's griping became too loud and insistent, Spencer calmly told the guy, "Hey, why don't we relax here? Let the kids play the game, the parents watch the game, and the official call the game."

Oh, another point. The other coach was not just yelling at the 12-year-old official. He was also hollering at some of the nine-year-old Verona players.

One more thing, Doug. The McFarland team was winning by three goals at halftime, which is like a 10-run lead in baseball.

And now we come to a young woman named Sara Desmond.

She's the head coach for the Verona team. Even though the other coach was angry and shouting—and her team was behind—Sara thought the referee was doing a good job. He had missed a call or two, but nothing major.

Sara had sympathy for the young man in the striped shirt and told me later, "I thought the McFarland coach was being a jerk. He was trying to intimidate the kid."

The McFarland coach was 37 years old. It is not hard for a 37-year-old man to rattle a seventh grader.

Sara continued. "I don't know if he is a jerk 24 hours a day, but that day he was not out there being what a coach is about. He was not an adult that I want my kids to see as a role model."

Sara, it seems, still believes in adults as role models. Quite a concept.

At first, Sara counseled her players to ignore the distraction. "I just told our kids to play our game," she says. "Not to worry about anything else."

But things didn't improve even after assistant coach Jon Spencer spoke with the McFarland coach.

"He knew a little about the game," Spencer says. "But I wish I could have videotaped him and made him watch himself. You see how some people act and you think that young athletes would be better off if parents weren't allowed to come to games."

The McFarland coach's actions finally brought an extraordinary result.

Coach Sara Desmond snapped.

Without consulting any one she just walked onto the field and proclaimed, "I've had it. This is it. I will not play youth soccer when the parents cannot control themselves."

And then to everyone's surprise, she forfeited the game. The big tournament game.

Mark it down like this: "Game called on account of adults."

Sara huddled her surprised squad of nine-year-olds together and explained to them that they had done nothing wrong. She told them it was "a parent thing, not a kid thing."

It's interesting that Sara really is qualified to explain these concepts to children. She has a degree in elementary education and a three-year-old of her own.

Ever the cynic, and occasionally the smug ex-jock, I asked if she was merely frustrated by the fact her team was down 4-0 at the time.

Sara didn't hesitate. "I would have done it if we were winning. And I have never forfeited a game before."

The Verona Vipers coach went on to explain that she was not "just some homemaker out there." Turns out Ms. Desmond has been playing the game for 21 years. She competed in one of the first youth leagues in Madison. Played high school soccer at Edgewood. Named to the All-City team. Would have played college ball but had to work her way through school. She even married a Brit who has played the game all his life. And she still kicks the ball around, on two indoor teams, one outdoor.

Sara told me, "A person has few passions in life. Mine is soccer. I just wanted to give back to a game that has meant so much to me."

I asked Jon Spencer, her assistant, if Sara had consulted him prior to forfeiting the game. "No," Jon said. "She just did it."

Did he support her decision? "One hundred percent. Our kids learned a valuable lesson. She had the support of our kids' parents, too."

It's too easy to paint the other coach as the black hat. To be fair in writing about this, I called him. Seemed like a nice fellow. Surprisingly mild-mannered and well-intentioned. He admitted to yelling. Thought the ref was too young. Said he was trying to protect his kids.

But Sara Desmond was also trying to protect her kids. She, however, chose not to do it by ranting and raving. She didn't confuse screaming with coaching. She did it through action that taught her young charges a lesson about principles, behavior and a seemingly archaic value, sportsmanship.

I wonder what lessons the McFarland kids learned from their coach that day? A coach who said that he had no regrets and felt that Sara had "taken the game away from the kids."

Unfortunately, Doug, he did not seem to understand that the game had been taken away from the kids long before this small drama was played out. Long before the game was forfeited.

Long before Sara Desmond snapped.

Regards,
John

July 1994

PULLING THE LEVER

Dear Doug,

It is that time again.

Citizens gather at fire stations and elementary schools. The local cops, resplendent in their orange vests, direct the traffic at the busier polling places.

Older folks man the tables, checking the voter rolls, their earnest work giving deeper meaning to the term "senior citizen."

Harried anchors stand ready to call out the count. One or two even offer intelligent perspective. And they all long to be the first to declare the winner in the Rio mayoral race.

The voice of the republic is clearing its throat to speak.

And I will vote on the designated Tuesday this month.

I will stand in line, pass through the checkpoints, and pull the lever. Or push the pencil.

I'm a product of '50s Catholicism, so voting reminds me of confession; I dread going into the booth and feel relieved when it's over.

I have never attempted to figure out why I vote the way I do. This is as good a time as any to try. I hope you are taking notes, Doug. My insight may help clear up some of the gridlock and apathy that exists within our political system today.

First, I vote for the smartest candidate. There are way too many dumb people in government these days. I don't want to make things worse. I figure if a man or woman is smart, he or she might just get something done for The People.

But I don't want them to be over-educated. I do not want to become a civics experiment for some wild-haired econ professor.

I do look for the ability to get something done.

We need to generate some chop on the calm lake of government activity. I want a candidate who can make the fat-fannied, sweaty-faced, lazy-boned bureaucrats get out of their damn chairs and hustle. I don't care if the lady is a Democrat or a Republican, so long as she is energetic and can move something…anything…forward!

Build a road! Erect a bridge! For God's sake, get something done!

And I want a tax cut.

Another trait I favor is business experience. I like a candidate who has been successful in the real world. Someone who has run his own shop. A guy who has had employees and customers. An entrepreneur who has built a bootstrap enterprise with his own sweat and perseverance.

But, I don't want him to be too successful, because then he would become filthy rich. And I don't vote for millionaires. It's against our nation's traditions. I think the Constitution states, "Never trust a man whose biggest campaign contributor is himself."

And if it doesn't, it should.

Another virtue I look for in a candidate is passion.

I vote for a person who cares deeply about principles. I respect anyone who maintains the courage of their convictions, regardless of the pressures brought upon them. We need more politicians who are unafraid to take a stand. We must have more men and women willing to walk through the night with their heads held high, unafraid of the storm.

But I don't vote for extremists. They're incapable of compromise. They're kooks. Their glazed eyes make my skin crawl.

Another thing. I want a candidate who is an outsider, not a career power junkie. A fellow citizen who speaks for the little people is the one who will get my vote, not the fat-jowled lobbyists and big money boys. Fresh perspective. New blood. Mr./Ms. Smith goes to Washington/Madison, and kicks some serious butt. That's what government needs!

A candidate who is too pretty will not get my vote. Neither will one with bad teeth.

I want someone strong on crime. More cops on the street. Throw the bastards in the slammer. Just keep building prisons.

I also want someone who can help me fix a speeding ticket.

I want a true patriot who will make sure that America remains the arsenal of freedom. Petty dictators and anarchists beware! Our tanks should be ready to roll any time. Anywhere.

But I do not want my son or daughters dying in some faraway land. Nothing, absolutely nothing, is worth that price.

I want a candidate who is Pro-Choice and against abortion.

I want a candidate who is an honest, involved member of the community. But don't try to run that Scout Leader-Chamber of Commerce-Rotarian-Zor-Shrine-camel-patrol-parish-elder-working-with-the-homeless stuff by me. You can't trust that type any farther than you can throw a voting booth.

I would support a candidate who has smoked pot but doesn't remember.

I want a politician who is a friend of the family farmer. But he must also understand that it is intolerable to pay someone a lot of my tax money to not grow something when people around the world are hungry.

As for capital punishment, I do not think the government should be in the business of killing people. Except for the guy who kidnapped and murdered that young girl from Waupaca. He should be publicly executed.

I want a candidate sensitive to social issues. A caring human being in touch with the democratic ideals of our country. A man or woman who knows that a government is only as healthy as its most needy citizens.

I also demand wholesale social security and welfare reform. There should be no free breakfast, lunch or dinner.

The person who gets my vote has to be a team player. Someone who can work with my guys. A candidate whose platform is consistent with other candidates who have garnered my vote.

That team includes Scott Klug, Russ Feingold, George Bush and Jesse Jackson.

And most importantly, I want a candidate who will assure me that my trash will be collected, my streets never neglected, and our borders, rights and personal health will always, at all times, be protected.

Oh. And I want less government.

Regards,
John

November 1994

CHRISTMAS LOST — AND FOUND

Dear Doug,

Driving north for a late autumn getaway, I spied the first sign. At the Merrill exit, where Highway 51 narrows to two lanes, a large lumber truck blew past in the oncoming lane.

He was not hauling pulp or plywood.

He was carrying Christmas.

Balsams and Scotch Pines bound for the tree lots of Madison.

And so it begins. The parties, the shopping, the decorating, all done to the soundtrack of Crosby, Mathis, Charlie Brown and the Mormon Tabernacle Choir.

And the annual challenge begins too. For amid the colors of green, red, silver and gold, I must contend with another color.

And that hue is blue.

Yeah, Doug, I suffer from the seasonal malady called "The Christmas Blues."

To get to the root of this condition, allow me the indulgence of a bit of self-psychoanalysis.

I loved Christmas as a child. Our home was always warm. The presents were always wonderful. The snow was always deep. And Santa and Rudolph always took a bite out of their cookie and carrot. There are no sad memories for me. Christmas was absolutely my favorite time of the year.

True magic.

But with age, the magic faded.

Work was one reason. I moved to Chicago and began my life as an independent adult. A high-pressure job during my years in the Loop took the luster off the season.

Deadlines, final details, late hours and jaw-grinding anxiety don't put you in the mood to go caroling. It was always a battle to complete each task, buy presents, jump in the car and arrive home just in time for Christmas Eve festivities. Christmas became associated with mad panic.

And money was an issue.

There was always the desire to buy something nice for everyone in the family; to somehow state with my gifts just how I felt about the most important people in my life. I wanted to hear that gush of surprise and appreciation; wanted loved ones to know that, although I didn't often state it, I cared.

My wife Diane and I would disagree about my Christmas spending. I was reminded that I couldn't afford what I wanted to buy. Christmas came to mean arguments about income and spending. Sometimes our ride home to Madison on Christmas would be, literally, a silent night.

And home was not always a haven. Each year the clan grew larger, swallowing up our own little nuclear family. Christmas dinner became louder and more crowded. Instead of the quiet murmur of conversation and music, the gatherings became a cacophony of crying children, noisy toys and Nintendo beeps. Above the din, harried adults talked in a shout. It is hard to experience the magic of Christmas when you are bellowing, "I THINK LITTLE JOHNNY PUT A CHRISTMAS TREE BULB IN HIS MOUTH! CALL 911! AND PASS THE MASHED POTATOES!"

Occupational pressure, money worries and sensory overload almost ruined Christmas for me. But they were merely symptoms. There was a deeper reason why I lost the Christmas feeling.

Truth is, Doug, I became a cynic. Lost my innocence. And so did Christmas.

The season lost its virtue for me when they invented shopping malls.

It was no longer a holiday. It became a marketing event. The mallers skillfully exploited the sounds, sights and soul of our collective childhood Christmases in order to move product. This was no local shop with warm sights, smells and personal touches. This was Corporate Christmas under one big climate-controlled roof with unhappy, frazzled, impersonal clerks and droning Christmas Muzak from Halloween through the New Year.

In this respect, I didn't change. Christmas did.

My cynicism came in the spiritual underpinnings of the season. When I was a child, I went to Christmas Mass with no doubts about the ritual. But as I grew older, the religious significance of the holiday became diluted by the complicated matters of faith.

Although virtue and values are now acceptable topics of national discussion, I don't care for the public proclamation of religious beliefs. But this much seems true: It is hard to have the true Christmas spirit without the spiritual. Christmas requires a touch of the divine.

All of these factors culminated five years ago in a truly miserable holiday. If I wasn't surly, I was catatonic. I know it bothered my wife. And I think it bothered my kids.

So I decided to do something about it. To recapture the Christmas feeling I had lost.

First, I tried to get work under control. This is not always possible, but last year I took time off on the 23rd and 24th. It helped.

Second, I buy fewer presents. No one has noticed. And I avoid the malls. Along the way I discovered that most catalog operators and small shop owners are really nice folks. They actually appreciate the business.

Third, we have our family gatherings in bigger houses. And we don't stay as long.

Fourth, we escape. We go up to The Woods and back in time. We try to find a little Peace on Earth.

We depart on Christmas Eve. Just the five of us. Corny as it may sound, we walk back into the forest and cut down our own tree. The kids decorate it with popcorn, cranberries and anything else they can throw on it.

No TV. No bowl games. The kids skate and sled. The fire blazes. Diane and I actually talk to each other. I also read and quietly play an exquisite tape of old Christmas tunes put together by a Chicago friend, who made it as an antidote for my holiday blues.

It all makes for a little piece of peace on earth.
Oh, and we have started to do one more thing.
On Christmas Eve, the kids stand in front of the fireplace.
Each one is assigned a few sentences.
And then, aloud, they read the Gospel according to St. Luke.
Not bad for a cynic.
Have a Merry Christmas, Doug.

Regards,
John

December 1994

THE SOUNDS OF SILENCE

Dear Doug,

Diane bought the Elvis clock when we moved into our little cabin. The hips swivel on the second, and the King's arms wave out the hour and minute. In the midst of the snow shoes, mounted fish and Indian blankets, it is refreshingly out of place.

And here's the coolest part: Although it is battery operated, I can hear it ticking.

I can also hear the winter wind blowing through the bare tree limbs and the shifting lake ice moaning in the dark. I hear the cabin creak, a bird call, a rustle in the woods.

These things are heard because for a few days this week, I have managed to capture a commodity that has become rare and valuable in the America of the '90s.

It is a thing called solitude.

The Third Wave, the Information Era and the Digital Highway are rushing to us. Our world is changing faster than our ability to comprehend the alterations.

And it comes at the expense of solitude.

Direct Broadcast satellite dishes now let anyone glom onto hundreds of distractions any time of the day. These stations don't play *The Star Spangled Banner* at midnight and go dark. They are a constant. An inconspicuous 12-inch dish can capture digital signals from the cosmic drift and beam them into your living room, kitchen, patio and basement. At any time, you can know the temperature in Tulsa, the total number of rebounds grabbed by the Charlotte Hornets or the fatality count in a Malaysian flood. You can watch *Citizen Kane* or disingenuous and shrilly-energetic infohosts urging you to buy hair gel, car wax, belly tighteners and cheap jewelry.

And they never go away. Once you turn them on, they have access to you. They will communicate non-stop information until your vision blurs, your brain throws a circuit breaker and you kill your remote.

The dish and the tube let these guys into your office.

Others have access to you. Too much access.

Friends, relatives, business associates and strangers can call you on the phone. Leave a message on your machine. Beep you. Call you in the car. Call you on the portable cellular. Leave you a voice mail and email, a note on your Newton or a message on an on-line bulletin board.

And they can drop exotic, hybrid messages. A voice mail to the car phone. A fax to your computer on the plane.

If they want you, they can find you. If you let them, they will reach out and touch you—and touch you, and touch you.

If it were sex, we'd all be trollops.

I suffer these intrusions poorly. I am too sensitive to the

stimulation. Things get too damn frantic. I lose track of the names, the places, the conversations I had. The jaw gets tight, sleep is unsettled. I become testy with loved ones.

It is time to take a break from civilization.

This is not unusual. Humans have a need for isolation. History shows us that prehistoric man, the saints and the Indian braves all had that innate desire to get away from The Nashville Network.

Some people fear this solitude. They are addicted to the drone of traffic and the distant scream of sirens. They need the constant din of human activity.

I once brought some Chicago friends to my lake cabin. Tough, smart guys. We arrived late on a moonless night—pitch-black and still as stone. There was joking banter as we pulled in the drive, the headlights cutting through the trees. But my guests turned silent as we killed the engine and headlights. We stood outside and looked up at the sky, hearing only the ticking of the car engine as it cooled. My friends were threatened by the silence and the dark. They were afraid.

"Too quiet, man. Too dark," one of them whimpered. He scurried inside and turned on every light in the cabin. Then he fired up the boom box.

He was afraid because he was face-to-face with the primal uncertainty that the buzz of Chicago never lets you face; the dark, silent woods. You see these types all the time up north. They can't deal with the silence. They have to crank up the ATV, the chain saw, the jet ski or the snowmobile.

They are afraid of the voices. Afraid of what they will hear.

They never catch the noise of the natural world. The comforting, organic sounds that are drowned out by the modern, man-made cacophony.

Those sounds that only solitude allows you to hear.

Isolation is not just an auditory experience. It is social too. My favorite thing about being alone is that I become the stripped down, spare, essential me. For a few days of solo living, I am freed from my roles as husband, father, son, businessman, pal and marginally upright citizen. It takes a while, but I get to be human in the simplest, most uncluttered way.

And that is when I hear the most important sound of solitude. First it is a murmur. Then, after several hours of seclusion, I recognize it as the sound of a conversation.

A conversation that needs to take place.

The speaking voices become louder and more clearly audible until, over the hiss and crackle of the fire, I finally recognize them.

Both voices are mine.

And that conversation, at last, is me talking to me.

Regards,
John

January 1995

SHOCK THERAPY

Dear Doug,

It was a warm summer night. I was asleep on the third floor of our childhood home on Madison's west side, having gone to bed early, tired from two-a-day football practices and anticipating a scrimmage in Whitewater in the morning. My senior year in high school would begin in a week.

Even though it was over a mile away, the explosion was the loudest thing I had ever heard. The windows rattled. The house shook. Downstairs on the second floor, my mother sat bolt upright in bed, alarmed and frightened. Dad just rolled over and grumbled,

"I'll bet those damned students just blew up a building." Mom scolded him and told him he was nuts.

He wasn't. They did.

The sound I heard that night was David Fassnacht dying. Dr. Fassnacht, a husband and father, was the researcher Karleton Armstrong and his accomplices killed when they bombed the Army Math Research Center on campus that summer night. Although it was not their intention to take human life, the Armstrong Gang ended up killing Mr. Fassnacht to protest the killing of other human beings in Vietnam.

In the compelling book *Rads*, author Tom Bates tells of the Armstrong bunch driving out of town as the bomb, made with fertilizer and fuel oil and left inside a van, exploded alongside the ill-fated building. The bombers couldn't believe what they had done. As their getaway car sped west, accomplice David Fine was alternately crying and worrying about who would handle his *Capital Times* paper route.

My overall impression of the bombers described in the book was two-fold: One, they were utterly self-righteous; and two, they were nerds.

Killer nerds.

And now there has been a similar, more tragic incident. Again a fertilizer bomb has exploded in the Midwest. Again, the malignant logic.

Granted, the causes were different. And neither the Waco raid nor the Vietnam War were wonderful, shining moments in our nation's history. But violent, misguided government policy does not excuse a violent, misguided response.

Tim McVeigh and his accomplices allegedly exploded their bomb to avenge the death of Branch Davidians in Waco, Texas. They killed Oklahoma children to protest the death of Texas children.

What is that?

McVeigh and his gang seem to fit the same profile as the Madison bombers: Predatory Dorks.

The news media has profiled the whole gaggle of these militia guys, members of a variety of militia groups across the country. They slap some camo paint on their faces, lock and load their automatic weapons and waddle off into the woods mumbling cryptic things about the Constitution.

These guys and their politics are becoming too familiar. We know the type: angry, disenfranchised white males. The power that had once been their birthright regardless of talent or effort must now be shared with women and people of color. Most white guys can hack it, even like it. These guys couldn't.

What most people call change, these guys call conspiracy.

I figure we can do one of two things about these fellas with the Army surplus wardrobes. We can complain about the people who whip these troubled mopes into their paranoid frenzy...people like the dittohead god, demagogue and serial gorger Rush Limbaugh, convicted felon G. Gordon Liddy and the loathsome NRA.

Or we can *help* these goofy white guys.

I propose the latter, as it will be easier on the rights of the rest of us.

Let's face it, a lot of these Militia Men just need some healthy social interaction.

To put it succinctly, they need a *hobby*.

Sure, preparing for the One World Order Armageddon may be activity, but it really isn't a hobby.

So here is a laundry list of things I think these militia members should do to take their minds off the conspiracy theories buzzing around their camo-covered heads.

• Form a bowling team. People who bowl are always happy and never paranoid.

• Date a woman.

• Go to a Concert on the Square. Pick something up at Pasqual's on the way downtown. Then sit down and listen to some Bach on a still summer evening. The soft quality of the grass on the State Capitol grounds will make you feel better about how your tax dollars are being used. And you will notice fellow citizens sitting around having fun and not looking at all oppressed by federal, state, county or municipal government.

• Play golf. In the history of the Republic, no golfer has ever blown anyone up with a bomb. I was a history major. I know this stuff.

• Call that woman again. Ask her for another date. But this time before you go out, take a shower. Put on clean underwear. Iron your shirt. Slap on some Old Spice. Bring her some flowers. Take her to a nice restaurant. (Denny's doesn't count.)

• Sign up for a juggling class. It's hard to think of conspiracies, or much of anything else, with three balls in the air.

• Go to a City Council meeting and find out how our government really works. On second thought... don't.

• Go to a karaoke bar and sing *Love Train* by the O-Jays at the top of your lungs. Do not request *Deutschland Uber Alles*.

• Visit someone hospitalized with a gunshot wound. Look under the bandage.

• Videotape yourself playing Twister with the fat neighbors. Then order pizza, watch the tape and laugh like hell.

• Purchase a Garth Brooks shirt. Shove your big butt into some tight jeans. Then go line dancing at the Dry Bean Saloon. Get on the floor even if you don't know a single step. And take that woman you've been dating. Laugh at yourself. Buy a round of beers. And don't talk about claymore mines.

• Volunteer to answer phones every time WHA TV has a pledge night. You'll be working so often that you'll never have a spare minute to build a bomb.

- Take accordion lessons. It is impossible to plot an overthrow of the federal government while playing *Lady of Spain* on the old squeezebox.
- Go live in another country for a year. After a couple of weeks in that country, try marching around in combat gear with a loaded weapon. Utter insults against the state. Then look at your watch and time how long it takes for you to be tortured.
- Join a barbershop quartet. These guys are always happy. (If Hitler had been in a barbershop quartet, history would have been very different.)
- Remember that woman you've been dating? Ask her out one more time. Make her laugh. Sing *Love Train*, play the accordion and then juggle for her. Whisper to her how much you enjoy her company. Then let things take their natural course.

The next morning when your buddies from the Militia call inviting you to avenge the Waco Massacre, to prepare for the Upcoming One World Order Armageddon and/or to Build a Bomb, you can tell them what the rest of us want to tell them.

The rest of us who are appalled by the weaponry and half-baked conspiracy theories.

The rest of us who don't blame the government for our own personal failures.

The rest of us who have had enough blood.

Just whisper to your little militia pals on the other end of the line these three little words.

"Get a life."

Then hang up the phone, get out of bed and make breakfast for your new female friend.

And trade in the camouflage boxers for some Calvin Kleins.

Regards,
John

June 1995

■

MINOCQUA HOPE

Dear Doug,

We had been enjoying one of those mythic late-summer evenings that make up January's dreams.

We were at the cabin. Diane was preparing dinner. Young John and I were reading, looking up occasionally to watch the bluegill and trout surface feed on the still waters.

Kate and Maggie had set off in the paddle boat across the lake to their grandparents' place to pick up hamburger buns. Maggie, nine years old and our youngest daughter, was excited to be showing off her new hat. It was adorned with a silk sunflower. She looked just beautiful.

The scene was idyllic. In an instant, things turned.

I heard a high keening sound. Being a parent gives you the innate ability to instantly classify the sounds your children make, and this one was serious. I jumped up from my chair to look out at the lake. Kate was furiously paddling toward shore. Maggie's head was bent, her hands covering her face.

I yelled across the water, "What's wrong?" Diane echoed my call, but our oldest was focused on getting the boat to shore and couldn't hear above Maggie's shrill cries.

I ran down to the lake shore, jumped into the fishing boat and made the short trip across our little bay to the neighbors', where Kate and Mags had come ashore. Approaching the beach, I saw them leading Maggie to their cabin. There was blood running down her face.

Kate whispered to me as I made my way up to the neighbors' deck, "They hit her." And then I knew what had happened.

Having been one myself, I can fairly say that seventh grade boys often act like dumb animals. This was one of those times. Two of the neighbor boys had been hitting rocks out onto the water with firewood fashioned into bats. They were trying to impress the girls by landing a few of the big chunks of gravel near the paddle boat.

As we are jogging up to the neighbors' porch, Kate says, "Dad, it made such a loud noise, I thought they hit the boat. But it was Maggie's *head.*"

After heartfelt words of apology from the neighbors and the dumb animals, we set off with Maggie to the emergency room.

To the room that Fate fills every day.

We enter holding Maggie's hand. She has stopped crying. Her hair is matted and bloody where the stone cut her scalp, one inch into her hairline above the left eye. A clerk summons a nurse who looks at her quickly. Hallway triage. Since our daughter is not unconscious or losing a quart of blood a minute, we are banished to the waiting room.

Checking in after us is a tow-headed, two-year-old boy. He seems fine. Then mom holds up his left hand. It is swollen to three times its normal size. "Bee sting," she explains. After they determine that he is free from breathing difficulties, he too is sent to wait.

Diane handles the paperwork while Maggie and I pick our chairs in the waiting room.

A family from Milwaukee has just checked in their 78-year-old grandmother. Heart problem. She is wheeled quickly away. No waiting room for her. Husband and son handle the paperwork. They try to stifle their concern in Social Security numbers and small talk. More family arrives. Several doctors and nurses rush into her examining room and shut the door. There will be a long vigil for this clan. In another corner a smiling local slouches with an embarrassed smile. I can't peg his problem. Then I see his finger. A muskie hook is embedded deep in his middle digit. He grins and shrugs.

A young mother enters holding her babe in her arms. Another two-year-old. He had been on a swing set and had veered off course, raking his head against a protruding nail on the support posts. They get this young one into an examining room right away.

They finally call, "Maggie Roach." We are herded into a room marked "Suturing." They wash the wound. It is much deeper than we thought, more a puncture than a cut. I watch Diane's eyes. She winces and shakes her head.

I walk into the hallway. A helicopter appears through the window and lands. The staff talks grimly. "Possible C-spine injury." Paralysis. A child fell from a horse at summer camp near Rhinelander. I head back into the examining room where my daughter lies. I'm not sure I can bear to watch that horse-riding accident roll through the doors.

The doctor enters. Maggie makes her final arguments against stitches, but we assure her that the Novocain shot will not hurt. A solitary tear rolls down her cheek as the doc preps to sew.

With the anesthetic in effect, he is now able to probe the wound fully. Diane and I both see it at the same time. It is very white. It is bone. It is our daughter's skull.

"Whoa," the doctor said. "Looks like it's cut all the way down, but I see no sign of fracture here. Good thing she was wearing a hat."

If you can avoid seeing your child's skull, Doug, do so. Not easy to look at. Not easy to forget.

Beneath the surgical drapes, Maggie is unperturbed. She smiles gamely and says, "Dad, turn your head a little. I can see the cut reflected in your glasses. I'd rather not."

Our daughter is sewn up, with internal stitches around the membrane of the skull, as well as external stitches on the scalp. We are sent home with a warning to watch for infection.

Maggie handled the suturing better than the muskie-hooked fisherman before us. He nearly passed out. "Just can't stand shots," he explains, his face white and ashen. Maggie chuckles as they place his hook in the trophy case with the 500 other fishing lures they have removed this summer.

The emergency helicopter stands silent sentinel as we exit into the dark. Someone may lose their mother, their grandmother tonight. Somewhere a couple will get a call from camp. A call about their child, a fall from a horse and the words "spinal surgery."

The next day, our neighbors, concerned and guilt-ridden, give Mags a gift. It is a statue of an eagle balanced precariously on a limb.

She names it "Stitches."

Regards,
John

September 1995

A GIRL'S PLACE

Dear Doug,

It was one of life's cooler moments. The television strobe lit the living room as I performed my usual channel surf through the cable ether. Diane and the two youngest were asleep. Kate, our oldest, sat beside me.

She was wearing her Umbro soccer shorts and a T-shirt. Earlier today she and her soccer teammates had been ball girls at the UW women's soccer tournament. They got to be on the field with one of the most successful intercollegiate sports dynasties of all time, the North Carolina women's team.

Kate is becoming a young woman herself. She started seventh grade this fall. Diane reminds me that we have just six years left with our first born before she enters college.

Six more years to teach her what she needs to know.

Father and daughter watch as CNBC dissects the latest developments in the Simpson case. As ESPN tells us of the return of Monica Seles. As CNN carries news of the UN Women's Conference in China. As Headline News carries the aftermath of the Shannon Faulkner episode at the Citadel.

And then a commercial comes on. It catches the eye. A montage of young girls staring straight into the camera. They deliver a litany of facts and figures about women and sports.

I helped coach Kate's sixth-grade basketball team last year. Although I had some reservations about the time commitment, I wanted to do what I could to encourage her and her sister Maggie to compete in team sports.

The reason is simple.

I want my daughters to experience what my generation of women was largely denied: the experience of working and sweating together with other women. The thrill of accomplishing a group goal after weeks of hard work. The satisfaction of achievement that has no link to men or boys and their opinions of you.

The chance to do it instead of cheering for someone else who is.

As Kate and I watch, the commercial continues. The young, proud female subjects gaze into the camera with nary a blink. They declare a few facts about girls and women athletes.

Confidently, one proclaims a lower incidence of unwanted pregnancies among girls who compete in sports.

I have been in many business meetings where men from my generation have an unspoken advantage over women our age because we were taught the primal lessons of the group hunt.

We've been trained to recognize and instinctively use the team dynamics that sport teaches. How to spot a challenge and respond without apology.

How not to take it personally. How to get the ball to the guy who's hot.

How to know when a pivotal moment is upon you. When to leap. When to pounce. When not to blink. When to run.

And when to laugh it all off and move on to the next game.

I want my daughters to know this stuff.

And I want them to hold that private knowledge of self that sports can reveal. I want them to know what sweat can teach. That they can score that goal. Sink that last shot. Make the play. Be tough.

I want them to know that their bodies are strong.

Another young girl eyes the camera. She states that girls who play sports are less likely to tolerate spousal abuse.

I do not want my daughters to compete with boys. Even though their bodies are strong, the physics of muscle mass and speed make most girls vulnerable in competition with boys after the earliest grades. But I hope they don't feel the need to compete with boys.

I hope they find satisfaction and joy in their own she-jock culture, with their own codes of conduct and esprit, free from the male agenda but equal in its resources.

The commercial continues. Another young women turns to camera. She states that girls who play sports have a lower incidence of breast cancer. Kate and Maggie have a good role model in all of this, and it's not me.

It's their mom Diane and her sisters and friends. They play volleyball in one of the city leagues. They strap on knee pads to dive, spike and bump a couple nights a week. Gaining the strength that women garner when they get away from the guys. Showing their daughters how it's done.

Playing on the team they never had when they went to school.

The commercial ends with the open ended proposition that has been its recurring mantra, delivered by women of all colors. The chant is repeated again and again. "If you let me play sports..." The Nike swoosh logo comes up in silence and fades to black.

And then the moment.

Kate digests the commercial for an instant and proclaims, "Cool!" She spontaneously slaps me five from across the couch. We both smile. She gets up, pecks me on the cheek and heads up to bed.

And as she walks away from me, I notice a proud strut in the walk of the young woman who is my daughter.

Regards,
John

October 1995

GIVE US THIS DAY OUR DAILY STUFF

Dear Doug,

The last geese are stumbling their way south. The deer work the edges of the barren corn fields at dusk. The old bucks wait for the crack of the rifle they know is coming soon.

And older humans wait for the winter snows to cover the dead earth, hoping that next year's snows will not be covering them as well.

On the calendar, Halloween gives way to Thanksgiving.

It is a strange time of year to give thanks. The weird science of food production has led to a modem paradox: There has been a mass desertion of rural America, yet we have the luxury of taking our food for granted.

An abundant harvest is now a given, not a blessing.

Spring would be a better time to have Thanksgiving. We aren't grateful for food anymore, but who isn't truly thankful when winter is over? We've got all the soybeans we can use, but farmers and ag scientists still haven't figured out how to make February fun.

Ah well, someday.

In maudlin Irish fashion I do take a little time in the midst of the Holiday of Thanks and Gluttony to consider those things for which I am grateful. The health of my wife and children. Gainful employment. A full head of hair.

But in this highly rated city, in this pretty state, in this wealthy country, I hear that quiet, nagging voice whispering to me. And it keeps asking the same question:

"Do you really need all this crap?"

The whisper continues. Do I really need so much square footage on the cul-de-sac? That new set of golf clubs? The nice wheels? All those CDs? The second TV in the basement?

Did we really have to paint the walls in the bedroom?

How many bikes do we have in the garage now?

Wasn't there something in the fridge that was edible and paid for? Did we really have to order the 15 bucks worth of pizza that was brought to our door last night?

My latest daydream has been to live a simpler way. Like the

Pilgrims, only without the scurvy. To retreat from the life of a wanton American consumer. More than once in the last few months, after I have surveyed the charge card bills and taken the big exhale, I have turned to Diane and asked, "Should we just sell it all and move to the cabin?"

The joint in the woods is the one expense I don't regret. It is the life Up North that I most enjoy. It is primal. Simple. I catch fish and feed the family. We have less living space but get along better. We heat with firewood. The phone rings less.

And there is also no TV.

No TV urging us to buy all those things we don't need. All those objects that end up on a card table in May, ready for the garage sale. All those super soakers and cross-training shoes that scream, "Look at all the useless crap we bought in the last few years that we never used, don't like and didn't make us happy. Take it off our hands for 75 cents! Hell, you can have it for nothing. Just take it away!"

"And, no, the card table is not for sale. We need it for all the useless crap we're going to buy this year."

There is a jacket in my closet that I have never worn and was too lazy and distracted to return. I have two dress shirts that were purchased a year ago. They are still in their wrappers. I have several compact discs that I have only listened to once. And only to one song.

I am not the only consumer running amuck.

As we pray over the turkey and cranberry sauce, would it be ungrateful to flash on all the food we waste? It is amazing what Americans throw down the disposal or into the trash. Sometimes it seems that we toss more food than we eat. Those guys at Plymouth Rock could have lived for three winters on the vittles the average American family throws away in the evening.

This is not self-flagellating, Catholic, Midwestern guilt. Simply put, Americans consume. We are proud of it. We are the people who put useless fins on a Chevy and loved paying for it. We buy faster and in greater quantities than any other society on earth. But the whisper calls again, "Does it make you happy?"

It would seem that our American wealth would make most of us utterly giddy, but isn't the opposite true? Our consumer society is based upon the message that no matter what you have, it isn't enough. How can you be truly happy without the new Taurus? Honey Nut Cheerios instead of just plain old cereal? A more vivid home video camera with freeze frame?

After all, the neighbors just got one, and they love it.

And aren't we all just thrilled with the grinding work we must perform to purchase all these things that we don't need and don't make us happy beyond the two hours after purchase?

And so I pray over the stuffing. The Detroit Lions game blares on the big screen. Somewhere a Nintendo game chirps. The trash compactor groans. The CD player spins. And I am not thankful for any of these things. It is only the simpler things for which I feel truly grateful.

And a simpler life that I long for.

Regards,
John

November 1995

CARS, STARS AND ROCKET SHIPS

Dear Doug,

Remember my Christmas note of last year when I described my struggle with this season? Well, no whining this year. Instead I would like to regale you with the recollections of one of my more memorable Christmas Eves.

By the way Doug, do you speak Spanish?

It is the night before Christmas 1968. I am a junior in high school. It is 8:30 p.m. Our home is bedlam. Upstairs my younger sisters are fighting over panty hose. The two oldest boys are trying to knot our neckties. Dad, reeking of Old Spice, hovers behind us giving Half-Windsor help. Mom helps the two younger boys with clip-ons.

We are preparing to embark on a new family tradition. Midnight Mass.

We set out to join a few families at Holy Name Seminary for a quiet celebration. The night is clear and very cold. The snow is deep. The moon is full, large and brilliant. The car fills with the mist of eight souls breathing as we make the drive to the chapel.

The Seminary was far away in those days. There was no west-side suburban sprawl, just farmlands and a large, lonely building with a church spire reaching into the clear night of Christmas.

As we near the rear entrance of the Seminary Dad slows our new station wagon. Ahead a car is in a ditch, buried in snow. We pull over on the empty country road,

My father gets out to check the scene. After a few moments he waves for me and Bobby to come out and push. Happy to do the

work of men, we jump out of the car. We are in our Christmas
finery, but there is a job to do. Pushing cars out of the snow is an
All-American Male Act.

As we approach I hear my dad talking in a loud, slow voice.
And then it all makes sense.

There is a Mexican family in the car. They too are in a station
wagon, but it is old and rusted. The tires are bald. The young
children look out at us, their big brown eyes round with curiosity
and fear. They are not dressed warmly enough for a Wisconsin
winter. The mother and father comfort them and shrug at us in
embarrassment.

They don't speak English. We don't speak Spanish.

Dad continues to talk to them slowly, hoping his deliberate
delivery will miraculously enable them to understand English.
Bobby and I chuckle as Dad struggles to communicate.

Two more cars pull up to the scene. It is our friends, the
Chrysts and the Doyles. Two men exit and walk toward us. They
are the dads of the families joining us for Mass. The Chrysts are
next door neighbors and as close as blood relatives. George is my
high school football coach. John Doyle is the family dentist.

We now have four station wagons full of families idling on a
deserted road in the cold of Christmas.

"What the hell!" Dad announces, "We can damn near pick this
car up if we have to. Let's get 'er out of the ditch before we freeze to
death." He motions to the stranded family that we are going to
push. They nod in understanding and appreciation.

In coats, ties and dress shoes, we men wade into the snow
behind the car and lean shoulders to fender. "On three!" my dad
bellows over the bad muffler. The Mexican father, a stranger to
snow but familiar with the English word for three, guns the engine
full bore. It is to no avail. The tires cannot get a purchase.

My dad then makes the diagnosis that all Wisconsin men must
make some time in their lives. With great drama he announces,

"She's hung up. We're gonna have to rock 'er!" The Mexican father smiles out the window as Dad struggles to pantomime the intricate Wisconsin procedure of car rocking. Flummoxed, Dad turns to George Chryst and John Doyle and asks, "Does anyone know how to say 'reverse' in Spanish?"

John Doyle shrugs his shoulders and offers, "Ah... Reversa?" We chuckle and shiver.

"Hell, I'll just drive," my dad proclaims. He climbs into the stranded car as the other dad exits. The Mexican children look at my father in wonder and fear. Their mother smiles at her new driver uncomfortably. My mother rolls down our car window and yells, "What is your father doing?"

Again we place shoulder to fender. My dad guns the engine. John Doyle jokingly yells "Reversa! Forwarda!" at my dad as he rocks the car. George Chryst is dissolved in laughter as the car finally rolls out of the snow and onto the plowed pavement.

The stranded family joined us for Midnight Mass that evening.

Somehow Mom got their address. Christmas morning my folks wrapped up clothes and toys and dropped them off with the Family in the Snow.

Our family still talks about that holiday. "Reversa" still gets a laugh. John Doyle now does charity dental work in Eastern Europe. George Chryst died too young. We still see his family at the holidays.

More than religious services, gifts, or parties, it seems to me that Christmas is memories, Doug. And I remember that particular Christmas because of its adventure, humor and humanity.

And its magic.

On the way home Dad turned on the car radio. Instead of the usual holiday carol. WIBA carried a live Christmas Eve reading from three Apollo astronauts as they orbited the moon. They were the first men ever to circle the sphere that shined so brightly over our heads that Christmas night.

This moment is frozen in time for me. Each member of our family peering out through the frosted car windows in wonder at the Christmas moon as Frank Borman, James Lovell and Bill Anders read a passage from Genesis.

"Amazing," Dad whispered quietly. "Unbelievable," echoed Mom in awe.

And then the astronauts ended their reading from the stars with these words: "And from the crew of Apollo 8, we close with good night, good luck, Merry Christmas and God bless all of you. All of you on the Good Earth."

Merry Christmas, Doug.

Regards,
John

December 1995

1996

ICE STATION WOODCHUCK

Dear Doug,

My friend Mike is standing in front of me. The many layers of clothing hide any distinguishing features. There are the clunky Sorel boots. The insulated pants over two sets of insulated underwear. The cold-weather mask that hides his face. His head is topped with a flapped hat of polar fleece and a hood. The thermometer reads 45 below this morning.

The only part of his anatomy that is exposed to the elements are his eyes, and they are freezing shut. "Mike, your eyeballs are freezing," I inform him. After all, what are friends for?

"I know," comes his muffled response. "Yours are too."

Larry, Kev, Ron and Rino exit the cabin and join us. Our physical movements are comically limited by our many layers of clothing. We move slowly up the hill to the car.

"We look like astronauts making their way to the launch site," I mutter. As we struggle into the car, Larry lies on his back in the rear seat and begins toggling imaginary switches in the command module. "Houston we have a problem. We have lost contact with our toes."

It is early February. The Third Annual Ice Fishing Weekend.

We are not ice fishermen at all. That is the joke. We are ice fishing because it is exactly not what we ordinarily do.

That makes it stupid.

That makes it fun.

It is manly to do stupid things in groups with other stupid men. There is that primal urge in all men that makes us go off into the wilds and act really ignorant, boorish and flatulent for a few days. It gives us cause to miss our wives and children. Guys need these outings to remind us of how we used to live in college and why we stopped.

And now in this incredible cold in Northern Wisconsin, we are doing our male thing. I am smoking a cigar and drinking a beer right through my cold-weather face mask. You just have to suck a little harder.

Suddenly there is a call. "Flag!" We scurry out of the shack into the cold and shuffle to the hole. It is Ron's turn to try and set the hook. He drops to his knees as we look on. Slowly he retrieves the slack. "Not too fast," advises Mike. "Don't set the hook too hard," offers Rino. "Or too soft," says Kev.

"Now! Set it now!" I bark.

Ron misses the fish. He is disgraced. There is a multitude of reasons why he didn't take this fish, and we discuss them all. We have absolutely no idea what we are talking about. This, too, is very manly. Men will talk about golf swings, basketball players or football strategies forever. Utter ignorance bars no one from these discussions. Indeed, it is an asset as it keeps the conversation alive.

We return to the shanty and the rumor builds. Our ice fishing guide George has returned from his truck to retrieve a spatula to fry the fish we haven't caught, and while there he heard the phrase "coldest day of the century..." on one of the local radio reports.

"Do you mean to tell me that we are ice fishing on the coldest day of the century?" I ask. We trade glances, the truth coming to us slowly through our numbed senses.

"Wow. I always thought this was stupid, but this has gone way beyond just plain stupid," mutters Rino.

"If I die first, you guys have my permission to eat me to stay alive," says Mike solemnly.

"Not many guys can make the claim that they went ice fishing on the coldest day of the century," offers Ron, shaking his hooded head in amazement, overwhelmed by the enormity of it all.

"Your right about that," says George, the sage. "In fact, you can only say that once every hundred years."

"Good math, George," Kev affirms.

"Just look," I say. "No one on the ice but us and those two crazy idiots across the bay. Five years from now, there'll be the Woodstock Phenomenon. Everyone will claim they were here ice fishing on the coldest day of the century."

"Too bad the camera froze solid. We could take a picture," says Rino.

"Hey," says Larry from somewhere beneath his seven layers of clothing. "These conditions are perfect. You open a beer and it actually gets colder as you drink it! What a concept. In fact, think about it! This is as cold as you can drink a beer and as fresh as you can eat a fish."

All three of the advertising guys pull off their gloves and start searching for a pencil to write that line down. You'll hear it in a beer commercial next fall.

George mentions that it can't stay this cold forever. Already they are starting to take a few crappies through the ice in the shallows. A sign of spring. We nod as if we already knew this bit of natural lore. "Yeah! And pitchers and catchers report next week," I offer as I leave the warmth of the shanty.

The pale winter sun makes its way toward the horizon as I step off alone to appreciate the day. There has been confirmation. The radio said it was the coldest day in Wausau in the 20th Century. And that's an hour *south* of here!

We have done it. My chest swells with pride. What a remarkably stupid act! It's great to be a man. I draw a deep breath of satisfaction.

And then my mouth freezes shut.

Regards,
John

March 1996

SONGS IN THE KEY OF LIFE

Dear Doug,

Recently a person close to me had a serious cancer scare. In the midst of trying to garner the medical information that would eventually help us determine that things would be scary, but end happily, we had one of those conversations where you talk about everything that matters.

Near the end of the visit, this person got down to the heart of it.

"I don't want to die yet," she stated wryly. "I haven't even figured out if there's an afterlife!"

I chuckled and assured this person that, fortunately, medical science had advanced to the point where she could spend the next several decades considering the question.

As baby boomers and their parents age, the whole mortality (or immortality) issue has made its way into the forefront of the national debate. Our society is starting to take a closer look at death.

Let's face it, if George Burns can die, anyone can.

Some folks have a matter-of-fact attitude concerning their exit. My dad, for example. He has already purchased his cemetery plot and placed his head stone. The exact year of his departure is the only detail left undone.

Someone visiting the cemetery recently saw all of this. She called and asked in shock if my father was dead. "No," I responded. "He's just very organized."

My father is the exception, however. Most people still face death with fear and ignorance. Last month I was on the periphery of someone's passing. It offered some perspective.

It all started with piano lessons.

Diane, my bride and the perennial winner of our household's "Mother of the Year" award, determined that our second child, Maggie, had some musical talent and would benefit from piano lessons. Mom also surmised that Maggie was struggling a bit with her new braces and entry into fourth grade. Mom thought Mags needed to feel special. Piano lessons fit the bill.

And that is how our family met Sister Donna Kucenski, a member of the Sisters of St. Francis and a piano teacher.

Diane located her through a flyer from school and called. Donna informed my wife that she was taking students in her home, an apartment near our neighborhood. The date for Maggie's first lesson was set. There was a special circumstance, however.

"You should know," Sister Donna informed Diane, "that I am a

71

cancer patient." Diane was mildly concerned about the situation but proceeded. The night after the first lesson, I came home to the sounds of Mags banging away on the old, used upright in our basement. I asked Diane how things went, and she smiled. Maggie bounced up the steps to drag me back downstairs to hear her play. She told me that Sister Donna was very nice and had taught her a lot. And then Maggie played her first song for me. She finished, proud and beaming. Then she mentioned as an afterthought, "Oh, and I wore a mask."

Sister Donna explained the surgical mask for me when I accompanied Maggie to her next lesson. "I am undergoing chemotherapy, and my immune system is weakened," she informed me with an apologetic smile as she put on her mask. "If I am going to beat this cancer, I cannot afford to get the flu. I hope this is not a bother for you and Maggie." It didn't faze Mags a bit. She already had her face gear on and was seated at the piano in the small apartment which was immediately adjacent to a hospital bed.

As far as Maggie was concerned, everyone wore a surgical mask to play the piano.

The lessons proceeded over a year. There were times when our family's schedule or Sister Donna's health did not allow for the weekly instructions. The piano teacher's life was almost as complicated as ours.

She shared her apartment with two other religious sisters and her aging mother.

When the lessons couldn't be held, Sister Donna would always send instructions. Even when she was ill from her treatments or the progression of her illness, she would call and ask Maggie to play for her over the phone. She provided our daughter with constant encouragement and affection.

The months progressed. Maggie's piano playing improved, but Sister Donna's health did not. One night, a parent of one of Sister

Donna's other pupils called to ask that we pray for a surgical procedure that Donna was having the next morning. Donna's instructions were very specific. We were to pray for the doctors performing the procedure. We were given their exact names and how they were spelled. The piano teacher was as conscientious with God as she was with Maggie and her scales.

The lessons came less often in late winter of this year. Rather than prayers for her health, however, Sister Donna asked that everyone pray for her pupils' performance at a big recital in February. Some of her advanced students had chances for scholarships. Donna attended that recital in a wheelchair. It would be the last time she would see some of her students.

We got a call one morning in late March. Maggie's piano teacher was "struggling," and if anyone wanted to stop by for a visit for the last time, this might be the day. Before we finished discussing it, we got another call telling us that Sister Donna Kucenski had died at her home in bed. The bed I had seen beside her piano that day I had stayed for Maggie's lesson.

I think Sister Donna knew that our daughter Maggie might be the last new piano student of her life. I sometimes felt that she was pouring all she knew about music into Mags, while trying never to make things uncomfortable for her. She made Maggie feel very special.

In the end, Sister Donna taught much more than piano. She was a good and selfless soul. She honored and dignified life by performing her chosen work for others as well as she could for as long as she could. She gave knowledge with compassion. And she left this life with the enviable spiritual fortitude that those with strong faith possess.

If anyone can be holy, she was.

Public discourse will continue about the value of life and the existence of a human spirit. But as someone who struggles himself with these questions, I think Sister Donna gave me a gift. A sense, at least, of what the human soul might sound like.

I am listening to it now as I write.

It is the sound of a nine-year-old girl playing scales on an old piano.

Regards,
John

May 1996

■

THE OTHER "LOST GENERATION"

Dear Doug,

I leave a message on Mary's machine in Los Angeles. She is an old high school friend. She can return the call later. After the wake.

I tell her that another dad has passed away.

I turn left off Whitney Way onto Odana heading west. The car window is open to the warm spring evening. Other cars pull into the funeral home ahead of me.

John and I had been best friends in high school. He was the quarterback. I was the end. We shared stories about girls and unrealistic athletic dreams.

We wandered apart over the years, but as I pass through the receiving line in front of the casket holding his father, the images and sounds of those days and that friendship return in a rush of memory.

John will bury his father tomorrow.

I tell John that I will not forget his dad's quiet dignity and his constant, still presence in the bleachers at the games. He was proud of his son but never made a lot of noise about it.

Sometimes, when we were sprawled around the rec room, John's dad would sit down to talk and laugh with us. He would treat us like men. Just as Mike's dad would.

Mike was also a high school friend. His father passed away two years ago. Michael's dad was a boisterous, bigger-than-life Irishman. He loved to come down into the basement at their home and razz us while we listened to the Hollies and played pool. Despite our age, he too treated us with the respect that men accord other men. I was out of town when Mike's dad died. It haunts me still that I missed his funeral.

Back in L.A., I know that Mary will be affected by my phone message. She still tries to make it back home every spring to plant her dad's garden. She toils alone in the soil, since he died three years ago in his sleep.

A generation is exiting. The men and women who literally spawned the baby boom generation are nearing the ends of their lives. And, as any actuary will tell you, it is the men who are departing first.

They lived through interesting times, these dads. They were bred to rule their families and businesses, only to discover in their later years that the power they inherited was deemed illegitimate by many.

These men were forced to confront the fact that being a dominant white male was no longer such a good thing. Depending on whom you talk to, this generation of guys was wholly responsible for racism, sexism, the war in Vietnam, pollution, red meat, cigarettes, politically incorrect jokes and polyester.

The generational caricature of these men is one of guys who never saw their children born. They expected the wife to stay at home with the kids. They wanted their pot roast ready by six.

They called the secretary "Dear."

Late in their lives, they wore their pants too high. Or too low. They were emotionally aloof. They would never cry.

But lately I have seen some of them weeping. I have seen them cry at memorial services on the beaches of Normandy, in the forests of The Bulge and on an island called Iwo Jima.

It seems that being a dominant white male wasn't fun for some of these guys. It killed some of them and left others haunted by their youthful memories. Memories that caused long-held tears to spill.

Although I have seen a few of them well up at the news of a new grandchild, these guys probably weren't as "sensitive" as the men of my generation. But the majority of them did have one trait that many of their touchy-feely sons lack.

They were responsible fathers.

The incidence of single-parent homes has risen dramatically in the last 20 years. The term "single-parent family" almost always means "single mother." The dads have split. They have wandered away from their children for a variety of reasons: imperfect marriages; pretty secretaries; self-absorbed, mid-life angst.

Unlike our fathers before us, the men of our generation are good at taking the path of least resistance. Too many men deem their children disposable.

In the neighborhood I grew up in, with the exception of one widower, there were no single-parent homes. Few of the marriages were flawless, but all the children had a mother and a father. "Wait until your father gets home!" was a constant and generally benign threat.

How many children long to hear that cry today?

Not long ago, I was having a beer with my youngest brother, Jim. The conversation meandered to the topic of our dad. Jim remembered one morning, just a year before our dad retired, when he awoke at 5 a.m. to see our father loading his sporting goods into his car, preparing to do the work he had done for 35 years. "Here he is," Jim described, "out on the street in the dark tying a pole vault to the side of the station wagon so he could drive to New Holstein and be there before 7:30 to deliver track-and-field gear to some coach before class. Dad worked hard. He's always taken pride in being a good provider."

A good provider. My father's generation delivered more than a paycheck with that primal male instinct; they also provided a simple, yet profound influence that so many homes in America desperately lack: a constant, responsible male presence.

So on this Father's Day, Doug, I propose a special toast to the generation of men that preceded us. Here's to the men who didn't leave their families. To the good providers who walked in the door at every day's end to be with their children.

To the admittedly flawed fellas who managed to honor the essential truth of manhood: that it takes only a moment to become a father, but a lifetime to be a dad.

Regards,
John

June 1996

GALLOPING GHOSTS

Dear Doug,

The gravel path to our cabin in Minocqua runs a half mile out to the county road. Then it's another 2.2 miles out to old Highway 51. Round trip nearly five and a half miles. Not a bad run for a 43-year-old.

I set out at a slow, steady speed. Better to finish than to be fast. Especially when you are trying to lose 30 pounds in one week.

But I am well motivated. Next week I will be attending my 25th high school reunion. I have to get down to my playing weight.

Or, at the very least, lose one chin.

I face this event with dread and curiosity. I have been to my other class reunions, and until the moment I get in the car, I consider not attending.

Such are my mixed memories of high school.

It is the juggle between who I was and what I am.

I am about a mile out on my run now. My muscles have warmed, and I've settled into a steady, tolerable rhythm.

We will all come strolling into the hall where the reunion takes place with our own special baggage. For some, teendom was the best of times. For others, it was a time of adolescent misery best forgotten. Some attend reunions to laugh with old friends. Others come to vanquish, or confront, personal ghosts.

We were the class of '71. A wild time in America. For guys, the lines between jock and freak were very clearly drawn. The length of your hair meant way too much.

Now, 25 years later, it will be the presence of any hair at all on our heads that will be the topic of conversation.

We will talk about our jobs and our families. Some will talk of their divorces. We will remember classmates who have died. Games that we played.

We will resurrect moments that we remember with crystalline recall, only to find out that others have no memory of the event at all. What seemed so important, embarrassing or thrilling to you so long ago holds nothing for anyone else. Such is the selective nature of memory and the strangeness of the teenage experience.

We will try to talk of our jobs, children and accomplishments without bragging.

GALLOPING GHOSTS

We will dance with our old flames while our spouses watch.
The DJ will relentlessly spin the ancient songs.
And we will marvel that it has been 25 years.
I am at the halfway point of my run. I turn back towards home.
The road is clear and my pace remains even. Lost in my thoughts, I
have never run quite this far before.
Memory is a strange thing. What was it William Faulkner said?
The past is never dead—it's not even past.
Perhaps it is that I have more to remember now, but when I'm
relaxed I will sit back in my favorite chair at the cabin and slip into
a sort of suspended animation. A dreamlike fugue state. And I will
see and smell and feel vivid moments from my past. I will actually
be in the moments of my youth. And I will feel the bittersweet
sentiment that memories kindle.
I have those very clear memories of my high school days,
despite the fact that a quarter of a century has passed. I remember
the fatigue of two-a-day football practices. The clear colors of game
nights. The bustle of the hallways between class. The slow dances.
The good teachers. The bad ones. The sound of my own breathing
as I wait in the blocks for the sound of the starter's pistol.
I remember the perfume of the girls and the length of the
skirts. And I recall the final days before graduation. The feeling of
accomplishment, liberation and relief. I longed to depart high
school so that I might define myself, free from the perceptions of
my classmates. Those same classmates that I'll be with this coming
Saturday night.
I think that is what happens to many of us: A little bit of who
we are, or aren't, is based on that haunting, defining American
experience that is high school.
So this Saturday night I will put on a shirt and tie, happy that
my complexion is now clear. I will drink a couple of beers too fast
because I will be a little nervous. I will do my best to recognize the

faces I reviewed in the yearbook. And I will talk and laugh with people who knew me 25 years ago.

Classmates who knew me well, and not at all.

Before I know it, my run is nearly over. I open my stride for the final 50 yards.

My head is up and I am carrying a little speed.

And then over the final few yards I sprint.

Like I used to do when I was 17.

Regards,
John

August 1996

STORM WARNING

Dear Doug,

According to the Weather Channel there is a Big Low hovering somewhere out there. It skulked across the border out of Canada last week.

Now it is percolating over the Rockies. Denver's gonna get hit. When it's good and ready The Low is going to trundle out onto the Great Plains. Over the Texas panhandle it's going to pick up some of that famous Gulf Moisture. And then we are going to be put on alert.

Three to six. Six to twelve. Or that phrase that raises the dead: "Twelve or more!"

You should know all of this by now, Doug, if you watch the Weather Channel for the Five Day Forecast, hang in for your Local

Conditions, and then remote over to Madison's own Certified
Meteorologists.

You see, Doug, weather is everywhere.

There is a strange button in my car, along side the dials that
control volume, bass and treble. On that button are the letters
"WB." Weather Button. I push it. On comes an unending National
Weather Service drone delivered by an erstwhile government
employee telling me incredible things about weather. The dew
point in Superior. The wind chill in Dubuque. The mean
temperature for the day. And, of course, the status of the Big Low.

There is just so much damn weather.

And the cloud gurus are very anxious to tell us about it. Some
forecasters can make three inches of snow in Madison in late
November sound like the Kennedy assassination. As you know,
Madison has been getting three inches of snow in late November
for quite some time, perhaps since the Pleistocene Era, but some of
our weather people are young, excitable and just out of weather
school.

So we receive warnings. Great snows, mighty hurricanes, One
Hundred Year Floods, and those crazy psychotic twisters. If it's
really bad a governor or a president will fly over the land and its
weather-ravaged citizens in a helicopter to view the mayhem. Just
like us, they love to gawk at Big Weather.

And then our elected officials return to their offices and listen
to people on the beach claim that they need government loans
from the rest of us because when they built their vacation home
they forgot that hurricanes hit Charleston about every five minutes.
No doubt these are people who bought their getaway condo with
taxpayer loans they got when their house drifted down to New
Orleans because they built on the Mississippi flood plain.

To make everything easier for these folks and to reduce all
these weather problems, I would like to tell people what I've
learned from watching the Weather Channel.

If you live on the ocean you will get hit by a hurricane.

If you live by a river your basement will flood.

If you live near a desert you will get a drought, then a wildfire.

If you live in a trailer park it is guaranteed that you will get hit by a tornado.

So if you don't want your home blown down, swept away, burned to charcoal or launched to the heavens, DON'T LIVE THERE! Duh!

If you do live there, stop asking us to loan you money. Watch the Weather Channel, for crying out loud. Even the two dumb fairy tale pigs can figure this one out! Something is going to happen to your house! It's only a matter of time! Get out now! And leave that bad sofa.

Because Weather is bigger than all of us. It is God tap-dancing on our modern, heavily scheduled world any damn time He/She feels like it. Got a big meeting in New York? A ball game in Waunakee? An Overeaters Anonymous meeting? Tough. God can tickle that Big Low and blizzard us back to the Stone Age and there's nothing your boss, coach or Richard Simmons can do about it.

And I revel in it. I love Big Weather. When the first snow storm of the season comes rolling across Nebraska and into Iowa, I become giddy, happy, child-like. I obsess on the local radar. Gaze at the mass of green as it makes its inexorable charge toward Madison. I mosey outside every five minutes to sniff the moisture in the air, check the change in the wind.

And I holler to the kids to witness the first flakes of winter.

They can all try to predict Big Weather, but they can't control it. And I love it for that. With her occasional Winter Storm Warnings, Flash Flood Watches and wailing tornado sirens, Dame Nature demands our attention and places our petty human affairs in their proper perspective.

When the Big Weather Eighteen-Inch Snowstorm hits,

neighbors actually talk to each other. Strangers aid strangers and smile. Our kids aren't shuttling off in minivans to the constant soccer games, hockey practices or basketball tryouts. Instead they sled on a small hill alongside our house with the neighborhood pack. Sometimes they actually come inside and drink hot chocolate by the fire. Just like in the movies.

For a few hours during the height of the storm we go back in time. It is not nineteen ninety-six but eighteen ninety-six.

But then the plows come. The first cars venture onto the streets. The meetings are rescheduled. And the Big Weather moves on.

But check the Five Day forecast. Let's set the time-lapsed satellite picture in motion. Out there in the Pacific. See those tightly-packed isobars. Could be a moisture-laden low sneaking into Canada. Better lay in some canned goods.

We're gonna have to keep an eye on this one.

Regards,
John

November 1996

1997

A CHEDDARHEAD IN
KING CLINTON'S COURT

Dear Doug,

What has The Republic come to?

It is a sorry thing when Our Government stoops to blatantly desperate measures in order to curry favor with its voters.

They screwed up with the savings and loan crisis, Waco, and issuing that commemorative postage stamp of Vince Lombardi without the gap in his teeth. Now they're trying to make up for all of that bungling by inviting me and my wife to Bill Clinton's Inauguration and White House Ball.

If they think I can be bought off with a couple of tickets to a dance they've got another think coming.

I will not let this obvious attempt at bribery affect my attitude. I will be forever vigilant.

In fact, here are a couple of things I'm going to discuss with Bill and Hillary right after the Razorback in Chief takes his hand off the Bible.

First, I'm going to ask them to enact federal legislation to make it a capital offense to drive too slowly in the passing lane on Madison's Beltline. This is a crisis that warrants mobilizing the National Guard. Any citizen or foreign student who insists on driving 18 mph in that lane will be pulled over by the militia and shot at the side of the road.

Following that they will be given a trial and traffic citation.

Once this legislation has been enacted and signed by Our Leader (probably before the Inaugural Ball if we can find a pen), I will then cover a few more topics with the 42nd president of the United States.

Legislation will be drafted and passed making all professional sports franchises exactly like our wonderful Green Bay Packers.

Every American team would become a not-for-profit organization owned by their respective cities, thus making individual owners like Al Davis, Art Modell and Marge Schott obsolete. Their jobs would be outsourced as well as their constant attempts to extort stadiums from the citizenry.

Won't it be fun to tell these folks that we're making some roster changes and they're the ones being cut?

This law will have an additional benefit. Every Election Day, citizens will be allowed to vote on who will be signed as free agents for their local team. At long last, 100 percent voter turnout will be guaranteed.

A few quick pieces of legislative business will follow. The following people will be deported for Crimes Against Public Taste: Madonna; Barbara Streisand; all daytime talk hosts except Oprah and Rosie O'Donnell; and of course, Michael Jackson.

I will arrange for the The First Couple to immediately reinstate WGN on TCI of Madison. As an added benefit, WGN will be forced by law to carry Cub games 24 hours a day. The president, at my urging, will also force TCI of Madison to: 1) Dump all shopping channels; 2) Have a real person answer their phone by the second ring; and 3) Generally behave as if they care about Madison viewers.

And a quaint stipulation of the new law: every Election Day, citizens will vote on TCI's contract renewal, right after they decide on the Brewers' new DH.

While at the Inauguration, Doug, I'm also going to grab a few folks and get some answers.

As I'm dancing the Macarena with Hillary I'm going to whisper, "Hey, what's the deal with that box of papers, anyhow?"

When I'm shuffling uncomfortably to a song that doesn't have suggestive lyrics I'm going to ask Tipper Gore if Al is going to get hair plugs for the 2000 campaign.

I don't want the President to dance with my wife, Doug, for reasons that are a matter of public record. But while I'm standing next to the President at the urinal I'll invite him to Madison for a round of golf at the Ridge. The foursome? The Prez, Chris Farley, Barry Alvarez and me. I can just see me and Bill stifling laughs while Farley keeps yelling, "FOR GOD'S SAKE, MAN, TAKE A KNEE!" during Barry's backswing.

I figure I'll see Newt at one of the balls. Why do I think this guy can't keep time on the dance floor? I'll bet there's a whole bunch of members of the Black Congressional Caucus hiding behind some pillar laughing their heads off while the speaker flails around to the grooves of *Love Train*.

I sure hope I see Donna Shalala at the White House Ball. She'll be shocked to see me and will wonder how I got tickets. I won't be able to tell her that Scott Klug and his charming wife Tess copped a few invites for us, because I'm afraid she'd stalk off in a partisan huff. But I'll just distract The Donna by breaking into the chicken dance. With her strong Badger roots, she'll have no choice but to cluck along.

If that doesn't get a big belly laugh out of Janet Reno, nothing will.

It's going to be glorious. A Cheddarhead in King Clinton's court.

When I am old I will be able to tell my grandchildren that I was there as history was made. I will tell them that I watched as The People confirmed their choice. Bestowed their blessing and prayers upon the one person amongst us that we selected to assume the most powerful, demanding job in the world.

A fellow citizen in whom we have placed our trust to make the right decisions for us and our families.

And I, a humble citizen of Madison, Wisconsin, will bear witness to it all.

But there is a question that lingers. Cause for concern and worry. A deep, troubled doubt that will hang over all the festivities in Washington, no matter how grand.

Maybe you can answer it for me, Doug.

They got any good fish fries out there?

Regards,
John

January 1997

THE D.C. DIARIES

Dear Doug,

As I wrote to you several weeks ago, this Cheddarhead scribe was invited to Washington for the Inauguration of William Jefferson Clinton. What follows is my minute-by-minute dispatch.

Saturday, Jan 18, 11:47 p.m. Return home from Frostiball. Wad up tuxedo and shove it gently into my duffel bag.

Sunday, Jan 19, 11 a.m. Depart Madison
11:08 a.m. Ascending to cruise altitude. Reassure wife that this is not a turboprop.
12:10 p.m. Chicago's United terminal. Food court. Two huge slices of pizza. Make mental note to adjust cummerbund.
1:40 p.m. Depart Chicago via 777 service to Washington Dulles. Used frequent flier points to bump up to first class. (Hey! How often do you get to go to an Inauguration?) Wife orders champagne and begins playing with seat controls, which feature a personal TV monitor, leg rest and lumbar support. After third champagne, fully reclined wife muses that maybe we should just cancel our hotel room and stay on plane.
4 p.m. Washington, D.C. Check into Omni Shoreham Hotel. Headline "Faded Glory." May have been a nice hotel in Harding's day but now resembles what the old Madison Loraine Hotel would look like if it still existed and went unrenovated for 11 presidents.
5 p.m.-midnight. Iron tux.

Monday, Jan. 20, 7 a.m. "Rise and shine, honey! We got us a president to inaugurate! Yee-hah!"

8 a.m. Make way to Rayburn Building to pick up tickets at office of our affable host, U.S. Congressman, the honorable Scott Klug. Difficult assignment as all streets in D.C. are blocked off so that high-school bands from Wyoming can rehearse bad marching versions of the Macarena. Spend 38 minutes listening to fragrant cabbie swear in Arabic.

9 a.m. Return to hotel. Begin dressing for the eight hours we will spend sitting outdoors in 30-degree weather at ceremony and parade.

9:30 a.m. Continue dressing.

10 a.m. Other members of Madison contingent arrive at our room. George and Marie Coletti, Gary and Mallory Gorman. Make embarrassing revelation to all that I have brought a Cheddarhead to sit on during ceremony and wear on parade route in honor of Super Bowl-bound Packers. Groans except from Mr. Gorman, who sheepishly admits that he, too, has brought a large dairy product to wear.

10:01 a.m. Quick exit poll reveals that I am only member of our party who actually voted for the man to be inaugurated today.

10:58 a.m. Arrive at Capitol grounds. Pass through security. Cheddarhead looked upon with suspicion by federal police.

10:59 a.m. Cavity search.

11 a.m. Ceremony begins. Beautiful gospel choir. The Capitol resplendent in all its bunting and glory. The heads of state at attention. The Republic at work. History.

11:05 a.m. Change seats for a better view

11:08 a.m. Change seats for a better view

11:15 a.m. Jessye Norman sings medley of American patriotic songs.

I enlist in Marines.

11:20 a.m. Bill Clinton takes oath of office as 42nd president of the United States of America. Bravo.

11:21 a.m. Twenty-one gun salute. Band plays. Change seats for better view.

11:30 a.m. Clinton speech. Short. Not the Gettysburg Address.

11:50 a.m. Ceremony ends. Mr. Gorman and I don Cheddarheads to celebrate. Make way down Mall to the parade seats. Everyone looks at us.

11:51 a.m. Fellow citizen yells, "Hey! Cheddarheads!" I respond. "Hail to the Cheese!"

11:52 a.m. Guy looks at Cheddarhead and asks with Southern accent, "Whut is thayat?" I respond, "It's a wedge to the 21st century."

11:53 a.m. "What's with you guys?" "We're curdish rebels!"

11:54 a.m. "Where are you guys from?" "Wisconsin, where 'Go, Pack!' means something completely different from what it means in Washington!"

11:55 a.m. "Why are you wearing those things?" "Because it's the American whey!"

11:56 a.m. Cheese jokes are getting tired, but hats are warm.

12:05 p.m. Pass Inaugural celeb Jimmy Smits, handsome star of *NYPD Blue*. He laughs his butt off at the Cheddarheads. You know Jim's butt. You've seen it on TV.

1 p.m. Arrive at seats for parade. Two hours early.

3 p.m. President's motorcade finally rounds corner onto Pennsylvania Avenue. First Family walks toward us. Chelsea spots our Cheddarheads, laughs, and grabs Dad and Mom. The leader of the free world traces a Cheddarhead around his own head and gives us the big thumb. Then the whole Clinton family laughs at our goofy yellow headwear in front of the entire nation! I am so proud.

3:01 p.m. *Washington Post* reporter interviews us about our brush with greatness. I use all my Cheddarhead jokes. None make it to press.

4 p.m. Return to hotel room. Thaw.

7:30 p.m. Attend one of the "exclusive 13" Inaugural Balls— the Midwestern Ball at the Smithsonian Air and Space Museum. Two thousand women with sore feet.

The Pres and First Lady stop early and dance three seconds to the taped strains of Nat King Cole's *Unforgettable*. They don't dance to the live band because it's REO Speedwagon, who proceed to prove that they are vapid, aging arena rockers by singing one of their few hits—*Time for Me to Fly*—without ever alluding to the fact that they are playing on a stage that is surrounded by the Wright Brother's plane, the Spirit of St. Louis, a Mercury capsule, and the Apollo 11 Command module. But their big hair was perfect.

10:40 p.m. Chat with Mad City Dems Rick Phelps, Hannah Rosenthal and the always cool Ben Sidran.

10:45 p.m. Depart ball as REO is singing *Riding the Storm Out*. They do not dedicate it to Bill's second term.

11:15 p.m. Return to the Omni Shoreham. Sleep right through the 2 a.m. lobby war between the Mid-Atlantic and Gay and Lesbian Ball participants, who throw punches after it is discovered that someone has completely botched the coat check claims. Not a shining Inaugural moment.

Tuesday, Jan. 21, 9 a.m. Meet the Honorable Scott for tour of Capitol. Wonderful art, great status, thrilling history. Best quote, Scott Klug: "The thing that I enjoy most is to simply watch people's faces when they see all this history for the first time." The Congressman pauses. "It's pretty cool."

10 a.m. And speaking of history...we sit in gallery of Congress as they debate Newt's fine.

11 a.m. We leave our Congressman so that he may do The People's business, unable to thank him enough for our invite.

11:30 a.m. Smithsonian Museum. View George Washington's uniform. He had a good tailor.

4:15 p.m. Meet with Secretary of Health and Human Services, Donna Shalala. She does not really care to discuss welfare reform, a Wisconsin gubernatorial bid or any other topic that befits one of the most powerful women in the world. What does The Donna really wish to discuss? Madison. The Badgers. Ron Dayne. The UW basketball teams. And the Packers in the Super Bowl. On her shelf is the game ball from the Rose Bowl. On her desk is a Packer "Dammit" doll. On her mind? Madison. Donna reveals that during her discussions with the President to re-up her cabinet position she asked if she could do the job from America's most Livable City. Bill laughed and declined her request to become our first virtual cabinet member. Hold on Donna—if cyberpol Al Gore becomes the next president, you become the first virtual VP.

6 p.m. In the fading haunting twilight, visit the Lincoln, Jefferson, Korean and Vietnam memorials. At the wall, find the name of Charles Le Bosquet, Madison, Wisconsin. Died 1969. He grew up five houses from me. God bless you, Charles. God bless America.

Regards,
John

March 1997

THE BOY ON THE CURB

Hi,

The early spring night is cool, but holds the promise of warmer evenings. The trees long to bud and leaf, if given half a warm chance. The disc player purrs in the background, as my wife and I tool along on a quiet street that runs parallel to Mineral Point Road on Madison's west side.

We are on our way to visit my parents. They live in a charming condo development. This community houses almost every couple who ever raised their children on the near west side of Madison in the '50s, '60s and '70s. The living spaces are perfectly designed. Just enough room for the kids and grandkids to visit and too little room for any of them to move back home.

We are nearing the entrance to the development when I see him. He is young, a man-child, maybe 13 or 14 years old. He is sitting on the terrace. We pass by him but something causes me to hitch. It might have been his posture, or the fleeting look on his face; one of those subtle universal signals that humans use and understand in an instant.

Something is wrong.

I slow the car, finally coming to a stop short of our turnoff. I turn and look back down the street. I see the boy rocking back and forth in a sitting position. I shift to reverse and begin to drive backwards.

To my wife's quizzical look I answer, "There's something wrong with that kid we just passed."

The car is even with him now. He looks up. There is a pained look on his face. The window comes down and I ask, "Are you OK?"

"I'm having an asthma attack," he gasps between breaths.

I get our of the car and walk to his side. "I have that problem too. I have an inhaler in the car and I can give you a ride to the urgent care center. It's just down the road."

He doesn't want my stuff or a trip to the clinic. "If you could just take me to where I'm staying. I have my medicine there. This has happened before."

I help him to the car, and my wife a nurse, talks to him in a soothing voice that she should patent. She offers to call his parents on our cell phone. But he says no.

We drive at his direction. He's a nice kid. Polite. "It's only four or five blocks from here."

"Are you sure we can't call your folks?" I persist. If this were my child I would want to hear about it pronto.

"I'm staying with some other people," he states vaguely.

I don't push it any further. Maybe his folks are out of town, or perhaps, in this era of non-traditional families, there is a more complicated relationship.

Block by block he gives us directions until we reach the apartment complex where he is staying. It is a low income housing development, one piece of Madison's scattered-site housing puzzle.

He directs us to a unit in the back corner of the complex. Now, just a few blocks from the luxury condo we were going to visit, we enter another world. There is a tattered sofa on a front lawn. An old rusted car sits unattended, with the hood open.

We pull into a parking space deep in the compound. I tell my wife that I'll run him inside. We trade glances and she nods. As I get out of the car and trigger the lock, we are eyed by the neighbors sitting on the stoops.

The many children running about stop and stare at us. As I lead the boy to this apartment, a group of older Hispanic males, adorned in jewelry and Nike suits, grows quiet.

"Right here," the boy says. The screen door is kicked in, the bug shield ripped. The main door hangs open and through it I see an older woman with a cane and disheveled hair. Two younger children are inside. A third older boy hangs in the entry way. There are boxes everywhere. My hope is that they are moving in or moving out. My fear is that this is how things always are.

To the woman's unfriendly gaze I stammer, "He is having an asthma attack.

We picked him up a few blocks away." The young boy slumps in and sits down.

The woman rummages around the boxes, finds a windbreaker and reaches into a pocket. She hands him an inhaler. "Here, use mine," she tells him curtly.

"It's the same as yours."

I stand awkwardly in the doorway for a few moments and then turn to leave.

At the last moment I catch the young boy's eye as he sits hunched in a chair amid the boxes, waiting for the inhaled mist to do its work. He nods at me, with a resigned expression. His eyes are too old, too sad, for so young a face. I raise my eyebrows to silently ask, "Are you going to be OK?" He offers a slight, hesitant nod.

I walk to the car. Over my shoulders the older kid yells a belated thank you. I wave a hand in acknowledgment.

We exit the housing complex in silence. Diane asks about the boy and the apartment. I tell her what I saw.

In just a few moments we are pulling into my parent's driveway in our familiar comfortable Madison. I tell my mother and father the story.

"He was a nice kid," I say.

"Those apartments are just down the road," my dad quietly observes.

Such a short drive.

So far away.

Two months have passed and the boy's farewell look still haunts me. It was a gaze that said more than "Thanks."

His were eyes that pleaded, "Can someone help me?"

And I wonder what to do.

Regards,
John

P.S. To those of you who read the back page of this magazine, you will notice that I have not addressed this note to it's usual recipient, Doug Moe. Doug and his longtime running mate Jim Selk said good-bye to the magazine last month. Doug has left to become the Herb Caen of *The Cap Times*. Jim has retired to play the horses and stroll around the Square looking dapper. To both of them I say, "Godspeed and thanks." Lest this get maudlin let me also say, "See you guys for lunch Friday at the Avenue. Round up the usual suspects." JR

July 1997

—

DUDE! YOU'RE LIKE, OLD

Brian,

It came upon me slowly.

A smirk from a young woman in a business meeting.

A walk down State Street on a summer's evening interrupted by a heavily pierced teen barking, "What are you staring at?"

An awkward exchange with another writer from this magazine who seemed to brand me as an insensitive lout.

But the picture has cleared. I understand. I am now one of the most dreaded, loathed, frightening, pathetic, mockable objects in our society.

Bless my cholesterol count, but I do think I have become a middle-aged white male.

When did this happen? Just a few months ago I was young, carefree, fun and unthreatening. I had just one chin.

Young children and old dogs would smile at me.

Lost women would ask me directions.

Nuns would wave and say "Bless you, my son."

But all that has changed. Now I am doomed to life in the middle ages.

All society now talks about my beer belly behind my back. They mock my enthusiastic references to Bachman Turner Overdrive. They think my golf shirts are dorky. (And chuckle snidely when I use the word "dorky.")

But my hair is not yet gray. How do these people know that I am a middle-aged white male?

Is it because I hold the menu in another Congressional district in order to read it?

Because I talk about golf and the stock market?

Because I'm always asking if someone has an Advil?

Or is it because I order a juicy cheeseburger at the business lunch while everyone else is having the shaved herb salad with cilantro.

Or maybe when I use the term "The Mick" and then have to explain that I was referring to Mickey Mantle and then have to explain that Mickey Mantle was a great player for the New York Yankees and then have to explain that the New York Yankees was a great baseball team and then have to explain that baseball is a game that used to be our national pastime.

There is that other sign of the white middle-aged male: the hitch in conversational rhythm when we search uncomfortably for the correct word to use when talking about Women, African-Americans, Hispanics, Gays, Lesbians and anything to do with the internet.

Please understand we now know that we must never offend anyone. We long to use the right word, lest we be subjected to public scorn or lawsuits. It's just that, at our age, we can't always remember which title is currently correct.

That is why some of us (never me, you understand) have momentary lapses and use words like "gals," "Blacks," "Mexicans," "a little different" and "whatchamacallit."

Although these words are not appropriate, they seem to be so much better than what came before them that we mistakenly think they're O.K.

And yet we still look at an attractive female and say awful things like, "Wow, wouldja look at her!"

Father forgive us, for we know not what we do.

That's just the kind of awful stuff that makes us social pariahs. Outcasts.

But as I make my way towards the early death that justly awaits middle-aged white males, I refuse to wallow in self-pity.

Primarily because there is nothing more pathetic than a self-pitying MAWM.

And because I see a few bright spots. Take current fashion for instance. A whole new generation of young people has made really baggy pants that reveal half your butt quite popular. Middle-aged white men have been wearing pants like this forever. So our trousers are cool.

And God bless Tiger Woods! He has made the game of MAWMs acceptable, even "happening"! These days you can't shank a drive onto the next fairway without hitting three rappers and the Artist Formerly Known as Prince.

And one of the hottest rock bands in the world is Madison's Garbage. I've seen their videos. I have more hair than all of them except the lead singer. And she's a chick…er, a woman.

Oh I almost forgot. Middle-aged white males do have three other things going for them.

Power, money and the occasional affection of middle-aged white females.

Hey. Maybe this won't be so bad after all.

Regards,
John

September 1997

1998

"IS THIS HEAVEN?"

Jim Selk, the founder of this magazine, died in November.
I was lucky to lunch with him on occasion.
I write this letter to him.

Dear Jim,

Just thought I'd tap out this missive as I did not get a chance to speak to you before your hasty departure.

You'll be happy to know that your memorial service was one of a kind, befitting a man of your stature. All the speakers managed to deify and mock you in the same breath. You would have been appalled and pleased.

You will not be surprised to hear that the Irish wept.

Of all the tributes, I was most struck by something Bill Stokes, your old running mate and former *Chicago Tribune* writer, did at the service. He recounted several of your more roguish episodes and then finished by playing an audiotape of very poor quality. It was Hemingway, one of your favorite writers, reading from his own works. Although it was recorded many years ago off Mexican radio it had an eerie tone that made me think that The Bearded One was actually reading it live from that post-life domain where the good writers gather for lunch.

I imagined you sitting there, goading him on as he recited the passage about a woman of mercenary virtue who charged her clients on a sliding scale according to their efficacy as lovers.

I could hear you chortling at this reading about a prostitute in the stately confines of the Madison Club. And at a memorial service no less!

The Hemingway tape caused me to consider who else you might be consorting with in that next world.

First of all, I can imagine your surprise that you found yourself in heaven. Your first words must have been, "There has been some sort of a mistake! Who do I see about this?"

But you dawdle as your glance catches the corner table. There, drinking and smoking to their hearts' delight, are Oscar Wilde, Gene Fowler, Lillian Hellman, Mike Royko, Gertrude Stein, Ernie Pyle and of all people, Roundy Coughlin.

Ernest rises, pulls up a chair and introduces you around. After the exchange you grin to the group, turn to Hemingway and say, "I'm sorry, I didn't catch your name." This brings down the table as they all know Papa can be a bit pompous. But even Hemingway laughs. Royko whispers to Hellman, "I told you this kid was good." Roundy says something that nobody understands.

As you sit down, Grace Kelly walks through the door, spies your group, asks for a chair and sits down beside you. Her thigh brushes yours as she crosses her legs. She looks you in the eye and demands that you order her a martini.

You hoarsely proclaim, "I could get used to heaven."

Stein whispers to Wilde, "Wait till Marilyn comes in; he'll pass out in his gin." Wilde slyly responds, "From what I hear of the guy, that won't be the first time."

I can see you as you settle into the conversation, Jim. As always, you pick your spots, counterpunching with your quick one-liners, or placing the discussion in exact perspective with the clever anecdote or a wonderfully apt quote.

I am sure you delight in reciting Hemingway back to himself.

At our lunches Jim, you were most often the one with answers. But this day you have a question. Finally you cannot contain yourself. You pose this query to the table.

"Could someone please tell me what the hell I'm doing in heaven?"

The table grows still. A few smile quietly, as Hemingway clears his throat.

"We all had the same question when we got here. And as best as we can figure, here is the answer." Ernest pauses for effect as Royko chuckles, shakes his head and takes a sip of beer.

Then Hemingway says, "You see Jim, it seems that heaven is for the honest."

Enjoy the lunch, Jim.

And know that we miss you at ours.

John

January 1998

EVERYBODY'S IRISH

My dear fellow Irishmen,

Looks like we sons and daughters of the Emerald Isle are favored by the masses this year. And isn't it a study that them that has scorned us now find us to be a most interesting race of folks?

First that transplanted Chicago dandy, Michael Flatley, river dances his way through every pledge drive in the country. Then Mrs. McCourt's son Frank shoves his quill across the page and right on to the national best-seller lists with *Angela's Ashes*, his mournful, mirthful tale of impoverished Irish youth.

And isn't his Ma in her heavenly perch the envy of the saints?

Even those heathens at public television and Disney joined the choir with their documentary series *The Irish*. Their pictures told the world of the blight, famine, disease and heartless nobles that have haunted our people like the devil his own self.

It seems we Irish are the envy of the world these days.

But beware the charlatan who claims that Irish blood courses red through his veins on this coming feast day of that great Saint Patrick, who with his staff and the grace of God drove the snakes from our green hills.

It's gettin' so you can't slop your Harp o'er the rim of yer glass without soiling the tweed vest of a fellow Celt. Of course no true Irishman would consider a wee ale stain a worry. More like the blessing of holy water to a babe at baptism, is what it is.

There are sure ways to figure if the fella by ya is a Paddy. Does he know the second verse of *Galway Bay*? When you proclaim a toast does he respond to your call of "Up the Irish…" with the quaint, subdued refrain, "The queen is a whore!" And most importantly, does the fella buy the next round and back you when the first punch flies?

For those of you who are confused, hoping that you have a bit of the Irish in you, but fearing that you don't and the devil knows, here is a test.

You will find your answers below.

1) Which country invented the telephone?

2) Many Mediterraneans claim that fella Frank Sinatra to be of Italian extraction, but with those blue eyes what country is he really from?

3) Unknown to most and denied by them lace curtain historians, what country really invented the automobile?

4) The Swiss Alps are one of the most beautiful sights in the world but where do those sorry hummocks wish they were located?

5) Where did the first light bulb glow upon the freckled face of a child?

6) Last name of swimsuit model "Kathy."

7) What country invented ruddy cheeks?

8) Nuclear power was first discovered in a peat field. And where would this field be located?

9) "John Kennedy was the greatest president in the history of the United States." Where are you most likely to hear this true opinion?

10) Barbra Streisand's real name is Maureen Herlihy. And where would her family be from?

11) From what country are the ancestors of American football legends Jim and LeRoy Kelly?

12) My great grandmother sipped poteen with a woman named Widow Gates. And to be sure what country would her great

grandson Bill return to if he were in dire straits and in need of work?

13) Where was Motown Records located before their offices were moved to Detroit? (And isn't Barry Gordy an Irish name if there ever was one?)

14) From what country does the questionable delicacy "lutefisk" originate?

15) And finally, where was the first potato mashed?

Happy St. Patrick's Day!

Regards,
John

Answers: 1) Ireland 2) Ireland 3) Ireland 4) Ireland 5) Ireland 6) Ireland 7) Ireland 8) Ireland 9) Ireland 10) Ireland 11) Ireland 12) Ireland 13) Ireland 14) Norway 15) Ireland

March 1998

ATHLETES AND BROTHERS

Brian,

There are times when sport isn't sport. It is a metaphor.

When a millionaire athlete strangles his coach, it confirms our worst fears about our society.

When a pampered college athlete plays four years, never graduates and can't read, it merely proves our suspicions.

When a former professional athlete slashes his wife's throat and leaves her and an acquaintance to die bleeding on the ground, yet he is exonerated because he could run with a football, we despair.

But then a kid from Middleton High School inbounds a basketball with six seconds left in the Wisconsin State High School basketball tournament.

The pass flies through the air the length of the court. It hangs for an instant. And then the smart, disciplined kids from Milwaukee Vincent converge on the ball and swat it away. There is a frantic scramble. A Middleton player retrieves the ball at half court with the clocking ticking past three seconds. He shoves the ball toward the basket and time stops. No one breathes.

The white Middleton kids in their black jerseys think, "Let it drop. Let it go in. We have played so well. We have been strong and smart. We have played as a team. We did not back down. Just let this shot drop."

And the black Milwaukee kids in their white jerseys think, "Please don't let that shot drop. We have played so hard. We have been strong and smart.

We have played as a team. We did not back down. Don't let this shot drop." And then the ball bangs high off the backboard and falls to the floor. The Middleton kids sag. The Milwaukee kids leap.

Moments later the crestfallen Middleton athletes accept their second-place medals and silver trophy at half court.

And now comes another metaphor. And another moment when sport becomes transcendent. And we witness a scene that will become Wisconsin lore.

The kids from Milwaukee Vincent move to center court to accept their first place medals. But as all-state player José Winston accepts his award, he does not run back to celebrate with his teammates. Instead he moves to the Middleton bench and hugs Chris Hogg and every other proud but despondent Middleton player. Each Milwaukee player follows, walking this gauntlet of mutual respect.

The entire Milwaukee Vincent team moves now to center court. They hold aloft the golden trophy that signifies their Wisconsin schoolboy championship.

And they kneel in reflection. And then one by one, the Milwaukee kids look to the Middleton kids. And they beckon them to join them.

And so together these young men, smart and tough and disciplined athletes all, kneel to honor each other and the game they have played.

And we who stand watching know they are brothers.

Regards,
John

May 1998

BE LIKE MIKE

Brian,

The set is a basketball court, lined by blue neon. Smoke wafts across the floor. Out of the mist, a young black man rises, hangs and then gracefully deposits a basketball through a hoop.

You've seen it a thousand times in commercials, but this might have been the first.

It is the early '80s. I was a producer for a late night television show in Chicago. One show segment required me to direct a mini-documentary on the marketing of a young basketball player in the midst of his rookie year in Chicago. The young athlete was shooting his first commercial for the Chicagoland Chevy dealers.

The kid's name was Michael Jordan.

Over the ensuing years I worked with Michael a number of times. I watched as he became the transcendent athlete of his time. I am too jaded for celebrity worship, but despite this bias, I am a Michael Jordan fan.

The last time I spent a day with Michael was last fall. He was shooting a commercial with Muhammad Ali. Amazingly, Michael had never met Ali. I asked Mike if Ali was the one person in the world who truly knew what Michael Jordan's life was like. He pondered, nodded and said, "Most probably. But Ali stands for more than me."

Vintage Michael. Acknowledging his place, but adding the right dose of humility and insight.

As MJ made his way through the NBA playoffs this year there was the common notion that this could be his last ride. As the Bulls progressed in their crusade we began to see montages of MJ's most memorable moves and moments. Some were cut to the catchy mantra, "If I could be like Mike."

But stop. Listen, children. What does it really take to be like Mike? After watching and working with him through the years, I have a few observations.

If you want to be like Mike, be like this:

Be smart. Michael's intelligence is what has made him a champion basketball player and businessman. Beyond his obvious talents, he has just plain outsmarted opponents on the court. His selection of advisers and business partners, including those Madison folks at Rayovac, has been a model of how to make smart, thoughtful decisions.

Be a worker. Jordan works hard. Wanna win? Wanna make some money? Wanna be like Mike? Sweat. Then sweat some more.

Be articulate. Michael's evolution as a communicator has been marvelous to behold. From a quiet kid out of North Carolina he has grown to be a regular on the All-Interview team. You want to be like Mike? Learn how to talk so that people, all people, can understand you.

Be dapper. Michael always shows up dressed as well or better than the occasion calls for. A good lesson for the slouching, gangsta baggy jeans set.

Be a pro. If you want to irritate Mr. Jordan, show up on the set unprepared to do your job. Try wasting time and see what happens. Michael has high expectations for himself and those around him. If you want to work with Mike, be prepared to be prepared.

Be comfortable with yourself. As simple as this may seem, it is important. Michael Jordan just plain loves being Michael Jordan. Not all people wear this mantle of themselves so well.

Be humble. It is a wonder to see how relaxed Michael Jordan is with his fame. Here is a guy who is Elvis. The Beatles. Babe Ruth. Ali. Yet he often shows up on the set solo. No entourage. He shakes hands. He smiles. He acknowledges you. He jokes. He listens. Nice guy. Very, very famous nice guy.

Be aware. Michael Jordan has always had a keen understanding of the moment he is in. Wanna be like Mike...get good at knowing what to do and recognizing when to do it.

Be committed. Michael Jordan is the greatest basketball player to ever play the game, his talent eclipsed only by his will to prevail. His offensive skills were outshone only by his willingness to play the gritty, unglamorous defensive game. Such dedication results in a whole lot of gaudy rings.

Be beautiful. The thing that is most impressive about Michael Jordan the first time you meet him is the one thing you cannot emulate: his physical being. Long, lean frame, winning smile, large fluid hands, zero body fat, and as Gene Siskel once observed, "a universally appealing iconography." I have a different way of saying it: Michael Jordan is what God had in mind when he created the human body.

Oh sure, Mike has his faults. My guess is that his wife and kids would like him around more, a constant for athletes and celebs. And it will be interesting to see what he does with his competitive zeal once basketball ceases to be his main outlet. Golf and the occasional bet may be too restrained for someone who is used to hitting the runner, stealing the inbounds pass and nailing the J from the top of the key for all the chocolate chip cookie dough.

Whatever he does, this much I know: I feel privileged to have watched him work.

And though I am usually loathe to tell my children to emulate any professional athlete, I wouldn't mind if they tried a little to be like Mike.

They know they'll never be Mike. They shouldn't want to be. But by trying to be like Mike, they just might end up being a better version of themselves.

Regards,
John

August 1998

RED MEAT

Hey Brian,

Is there anyone in your office?

Quick, close the door. Have them hold your calls. Sleep the Mac. Boy, do I have news for you!

You wanna know what the fuss is about? OK. Come closer. I'm gonna whisper one word to you. Here it is.

Meat.

Yeah…that's right, meat.

RED MEAT

After years of enjoying a strip, fillet or T-bone at some of
Madison's great steak joints, I am here to tell you that there is a
new sheriff in town.

Yup. Move over Smoky's and Mariner's, there's a new chop on
the block. And they are poised to knock you off.

This is big news.

I don't know about you Brian, but I inhale less red meat than I
used to. Now, like any educated American, I consume more
chicken, turkey and fish as they are deemed to be more healthy for
our hearts. Hell, sometimes I actually eat a meal without meat of
any kind.

Like, say…twice a year.

But although these steak alternatives may be healthy for your
heart, they are not great for your soul. Because a good steak satisfies
you in a way eggplant pasta never will.

When I was a kid, I would know that my father got a raise
because he would bring a nice big sirloin steak home to throw on
the fire. This was more than dinner, this was celebration. This was
reward. This was steak!

A good steak is imbued with emotional content that your
average grains and fowl lack. This is primordial. You gotta figure
our Neanderthal ancestors got a little more excited when they
bagged, dragged and burned a mastodon on the Weber than when
the boys walked back into the cave with a pigeon.

Because a pigeon won't get you through a tough winter.

Now, I know that there are folks who do not care for meat-
eating. Fine. Leaves more for me. Unless, of course, those animal
rightists get carried away and decide to break into the meat locker
to set all the New York strips free. Trust me vegans, those choice
cuts do not know how to live outside the kitchen. Most of them
would be hit by cars or eaten by construction workers before they
ever got back to the open fields.

So anyhow…like I was saying…there's a great new steak joint

in town. Maybe the best. It's got all the makings of a champion. Good drinks.

Dark walls. Big iceberg salads. Killer hunks of meat exquisitely prepared.

They even have white tablecloths!

And here's the best part. They make you feel welcome. They don't guilt you for enjoying some actual conversation with friends while eating. They don't hand you your bill while you're still chewing so that they can turn over your seat to some Iowa football fans.

And the crowd is a bit more contemporary than at some of the veteran meat joints in town. A younger, cosmopolitan feel. Sure, the crowd can get a little different after 10. After all, I've never seen a transvestite at Smoky's.

But then again…maybe I have.

So I'm sure you wanna know about this place. I got only one problem here Brian. If I tell you about this joint, then they will become overwhelmed with steak-lovers, too. I'll have to struggle to find parking and wait till 9 to be served at the Tornado Club.

But that will be OK.

I'll just go to Smoky's.

Regards,
John

October 1998

1999

MUTE POINT

Brian,

I first noticed the problem while sitting around a campfire last summer. My brother Jim had broken out his guitar and, as Irishmen are wont to do after a few beers, we began to warble into the moonlight.

I opened my mouth to chime in on a Neil Young ditty. But instead of my fair-to-middling tenor tones drifting over the lake, out came a tortured honk. My vocal range had been reduced to two very low notes, neither of them pleasing to the ear.

This condition soon spread to include my everyday speaking voice. I would open my mouth to make a point, a plea, a retort, a quip, a request or an interjection and nothing would come out except rushing air. It was like putting your foot on the accelerator after your car has slipped into neutral. Using my voice, which was all too easy for me, was now a chore.

But there was a benefit. For the first time in my life I was actually thinking before speaking.

Soon my voice was not my own. It became raspy and tortured. It got so that when I spoke, everyone in the room cleared their throats. The only good point was that two women at work told me it sounded sexy. I am convinced this was because I was simply talking less. After more than 40 years of yammering away on most any topic, I had finally become the strong silent type.

Finally I dashed over to see my good friend Ash, who actually knows about this stuff, as he is a doctor who peers down people's throats. Ash grabbed my tongue, pulled it well out of my mouth, stuck a mirror on a stick down my throat and told me to say "EEEEEEEE." Just before my gag reflex kicked in Ash said, "There it is." He let go of my tongue and it whiplashed back into my mouth like a window shade.

"You have a nodule on your vocal chord," the good doctor pronounced. After a few months of therapy showed no improvement, we decided to cut away the offending growth.

The surgery went swimmingly, but then came the most unique of experiences. As part of my post-operative convalescence I was placed on three days of total voice rest. Yes, Brian, due to that little, benign growth on my vocal chord, I was prevented from performing an act I had pretty much been doing nonstop since I was 2. Talking.

I had already learned that our voice is unique to us. When it is changed, it is akin to changing your appearance. Prior to my surgery most everyone I spoke to commented on my voice. It was as if I had a bandage over my nose. And I was not as effective communicating. I could not raise my voice for emphasis. I could not alter my inflection to convey irony, sarcasm or sympathy.

And then came total voice rest. I was reduced to playing charades full time. Occasionally I would scribble a few words on a pad of paper. When we were out in public, my lovely wife would have to explain to people that I was not being unfriendly, I was simply unable to speak. My younger sister called me on the phone to tell me all the things she had wanted to say without interruption.

And here is what I learned from my three days as a mute. I learned that I waste many words, and hear so few. I learned that not speaking is liberating. Phone calls you do not have to take. Uncomfortable conversations you are freed from having. I learned you gain the social power that comes with listening and the understanding nod. And I learned that people like you more if you do not engage in serial interruption, as I often do.

Of course the benefits of being mute are easier to enjoy knowing that you will only be one for three days. Were it a permanent condition I would surely miss talking to my children and singing along with Van Morrison on the car radio. The rest of it I am not so sure about.

I do know that for three days the world was a much quieter place. And that I benefited from my silence. As did others.

One woman who spied my condition said it pretty well. She smiled and sauntered over to me. Then she whispered in my ear:

"My father's favorite Marx brother was Harpo."

Regards,
John

January 1999

115

—

THE INVISIBLE WOMAN

Brian,

I am stuck in a hotel room in Raleigh, North Carolina, channel surfing through the strange world of daytime programming.

I stop at *Oprah*.

Ms. Winfrey has been trying to save the world lately. Her show has taken on a messianic quality as she commits herself to bettering the lives of her viewers—a novel concept for television programming, to be sure.

This show is about lost women. Not women who have been abducted or taken the wrong exit off the Beltline, but women who are lost in their own homes.

Their own lives.

There is a tight shot of an audience member. Her lower lip trembles. The predictable tear ambles down her cheek. She had a life at one time, she tells us, but she made the choice to stay at home to raise her children. She now feels as if she has vanished. She has become invisible.

You see Brian, this woman has no career. She is only a wife and mother.

In another time, society would have honored her for this commitment. Her task of mothering would have been enough to make her feel respected.

But so much more is expected of women these days.

I am reminded of a woman I know. Her husband works for the state. Her career is her family. She tours Madison in her seven-seat vehicle, running kids from soccer to dance to school to basketball to doctor's appointments. I told her once that I marveled at her ability to juggle all the kids and schedules.

She paused and told me with a wry smile that it was really nice to hear a compliment. "When I go to a business party with my husband, men and women come up to me and ask what I do. When I tell them that I am a full-time mom, they turn and walk away."

Now why is that? Anyone with a brain knows that staying home and raising kids is the toughest job in the world. It is a selfless task that demands a broad set of skills. Although husbands and children appreciate the work, its value seems diminished by society at large. At least that's how many of these invisible women feel.

Stay-at-home moms get few reminders of their societal worth. When I bought income continuation insurance several years ago, I also wanted to get a policy for my wife; should anything happen to her, the costs to our household would be overwhelming. Turns out my insurance company didn't offer such coverage for women who stay at home to raise their children.

And we wonder why the woman on *Oprah* feels invisible.

The profession of mothering and wife-ing isn't very exciting stuff. It's old news. Too traditional. Sure, stay-at-home moms work to provide a loving, safe, constant environment for their children and mate. But working moms and dads do the same thing—or at least hope to—plus write memos, increase market share by 1.6 percent, and help with that new product roll-out.

Besides, being a stay-at-home mom is a luxury that many working women and men envy. Most families require two incomes to stay ahead. So please, no whining about being housebound.

And let's remember, the National Organization for Women hasn't been doing all this work just so women can go to school, start the careers they have historically been denied and then drop out to care for their children and husbands. That is not what the struggle has been about.

The women's liberation battle has many fronts—the Glass Ceiling, Day Care, Birth Control, Lesbian Rights. NOW is hardly going to stage a fight for a more elevated, respected role for women as mothers, particularly middle-class moms in two-parent households. Sure, they respect a woman's right to make such a decision. But truly honor it? That could be politically sticky.

And if full-time mothers feel no cultural respect for their decision and their work…if they feel invisible…if they feel lost when the kids leave home and they are unable to rekindle their careers—well, such is the cost of liberation. Hey, you gotta break a few eggs to make an omelet.

In this year of 1999, when we examine the great influences of the century, I do not cast my vote for the invention of penicillin, the splitting of the atom or the walk on the moon. I cast my vote for the emancipation of women. This century has seen more than half of mankind's population move from being property to being people. We have yet to fully realize the profound effect this liberation will have on our world.

But it is ironic that as the Western world benefits from this new freedom, we have devalued the most important role women have played in the past: the creation of human beings who feel loved.

Of course, if 2-year-olds could hold press conferences about the role their mothers play in society, you might hear a different story.

And you can bet you wouldn't hear the word "invisible."

Regards,
John

February 1999

—

NATURE'S CALLING

Brian,

The Arboretum has always held a special place in my life.

As a child we knew that summer would soon arrive when my father took us on our annual drive through those beautiful woods to see and smell the lilacs as they bloomed.

Later our family moved to Vilas Avenue on the fringes of the nationally famous preserve. In high school the boys would run along its asphalt road to ready us for track and football.

On the morning of my wedding I jogged alone through those hallowed gardens contemplating the momentous nature of the day. I did the same thing the morning of my 25th high school reunion, proud that I could still run the circuit.

When visitors come to town, the local beauty spots I recommend are the lakes, the stunning UW campus, the Square and the Arboretum.

So you can imagine my surprise one morning last month. Like so many I still jog through the Arb. And like so many I had to heed the natural call that three cups of coffee can evoke.

The call that falls alphabetically between the letters O and Q.

I was preparing to scurry into the woods and answer that beckon in a most discreet fashion when a yellow truck pulled into the lot where I had parked prior to my lope. Lest this be a carload of nuns, I stopped en route to the planned activity for the sake of the aforementioned discretion.

But I was taken aback when the occupant of the vehicle

emerged and bellowed in a belligerent tone. "Oh yeah, buddy? I know what you were going to do!

That's just great. Why don't you go and do that in your own front lawn!"

It seems that the angry fellow worked for the Arboretum.

I was taken aback by the rude nature of his greeting. Rather than continue my attempt to relieve my growing discomfort, I walked over to the surly fellow. A difficult thing to do with one's legs crossed.

I introduced myself and asked him why he was so upset with me. Didn't he relieve himself in the woods when the need arose? Did he always trek back to the inconveniently located administrative offices to use the washroom?

"I sure do," he huffed. "It's the only break I get."

But we weren't talking about his terms of employment with the state, or the fact that I thought he was lying between his teeth. We were talking about a simple, natural act in a natural environment.

"Aren't you frustrated, as I am, by the lack of convenient toilet facilities in the Arboretum?" I calmly queried.

"Why don't you take that up with Tommy Thompson?" he barked at me. I guess only the governor of the state can make these decisions.

I suggested that deer, raccoon, squirrels and other wildlife regularly tinkled among the trees. Yet the woods still stand. I told him that I know countless joggers, men and women, who regularly take a quick detour into the timber. I'd bet that even Aldo Leopold, the famed visionary who created the Arboretum, had actually relieved himself amongst the oaks.

The activity we were debating, as I see it, is both an inalienable right and a natural act. After three cups of coffee it is actually more natural, and more important, than breathing.

But the unhappy fellow would hear none of it. So I jogged

around the bend. Once out of his sight I ducked into the woods to do what had him so...er...PO'ed.

As I continued my jog through one of the most beautiful stretches in all of Wisconsin, I considered the attitude of the unhappy tree-pruner. While doing so I passed the many signs that boldly pronounce all the things that are prohibited in the Arboretum.

"No Dogs!" "No Skateboards!" "No Roller Blades!" "This Is Prohibited! "That Is Prohibited!" Big letters, with sinister state statute numbers that tell us that so much is forbidden.

I did, however, fail to find a single sign that says that you can't pee in the woods.

I also failed to find a sign that simply says "Welcome to the Arboretum. Please enjoy yourself."

It hardly makes a taxpayer feel welcome.

What's more, you can no longer tour the length of the Arboretum by car as our family did for so many years. I guess folks liked the drive too much.

As I ended my run, I looked for the worker who was so upset with me. I wanted to share with him the conclusions that I had come to while pondering the incident. But he was nowhere to be found.

Perhaps he was on break.

I wanted to respond to his initial statement, the one advising me to return to my own lawn.

He failed to understand one important thing.

The lawn I was on was mine.

Regards,
John

May 1999

CHEESE WHIZZES

Brian,

I have never been a fan of the French.

A recent Miller High Life commercial best captured my attitude toward our Gallic brothers and sisters. It shows the dirty hands of a fellow preparing a sandwich, a can of beer on the counter. The voice over intones, "Hard to respect the French when you've had to bail 'em out of two big ones in one century."

There is a pause and the narrative continues. "But you gotta hand it to 'em on mayonnaise."

A final grudging compliment ends the spot.

"Way to go, Pierre."

Recently my attitude toward the French changed dramatically. This can be traced to the fact that I actually visited France. What I found shocked and staggered me. An awful, dirty secret was revealed. When made public (which I will do four paragraphs from now) it will cause widespread panic in our city and state. A special session of the Legislature will have to be convened.

You see, fellow Wisconsinites; France is kicking our butts. They are doing to us what the Germans did to them.

It's not the exotic allure of the topless beaches on the Riviera. It's not the stunning history of the Roman ruins. It's not even the fact that French men and women wear really nice clothes all the time. Markedly better fashions than you would find at say, Noah's Ark.

No, my friends, the French are beating us at something we

thought we did better than anyone else in the world.

They are outcheesing us.

Worse yet, and even harder to believe, they are outbuttering us too.

· Yes, fellow Badgers, the cheese and butter in France is better than Wisconsin cheese and butter.

Stop! Before you call me a traitor to my people, let me say that I love my home state. I worked on a dairy farm. I send boxes of Wisconsin cheese to people all the time. So you can imagine my shock and dismay when my wife and I sat down to our first meal in France.

Suffering from jet lag, we opted to eat at the outdoor cafe of our hotel. Nothing could prepare me for what I discovered as we began our repast.

A basket of bread was brought to our table. (By the way, their bread is tremendous, too.) I took my knife and spread a bit of butter on the baguette. I placed the morsel casually in my mouth as I conversed with my bride. And then, as my taste buds processed the sensory information, I stopped in midsentence.

"My God!" I exclaimed, "This bread tastes great. And this butter! This butter is delicious!"

"You should try the cheese!" Diane cried, picking up on the theme as she wolfed down her third slice of brie.

This was not a solitary incident. Throughout the week we were amazed by the quality of the French food in general, and the sweet, rich taste of their cheese and butter specifically.

Mine was not a voice in the wilderness. We were in the company of a number of Wisconsin folk. In hushed, concerned voices they all agreed that the French cheese and butter tasted better than ours. But why?

Upon our return I quietly queried a few folks concerning this phenomenon.

"Their grasses are sweeter," explained my professor friend. "Plus they use fewer chemicals on their cows."

"It's their Brown Swiss cows. Their milk has higher butterfat content," stated my neighbor succinctly.

I asked a few more Badgers in the know.

"They don't wrap their cheese in plastic. They let it breathe."

"They serve it at room temperature. This heightens the aroma."

And what about the butter?

"I don't know why French butter tastes better than ours," answered one world traveler, "but New Zealand's butter is even better than France's."

A friend offered a final opinion. "There's a simple explanation why you thought French cheese and butter tasted better than ours." He paused. "Because you were in France, stupid."

Regards,
John

July 1999

━

JOHNNY'S SONG

Brian,

We are in a van heading back from Waukesha. Two dads sit in front while the pack of recently graduated fifth grade boys laugh and giggle in back. It is a loose-knit bunch of kids from a couple of schools.

They've all got the basketball jones. This is the bus ride home after three tough games.

It is our family's first experience with a traveling team. Son John's older sisters play basketball, though most of their youthful contests have taken place in the 608 area code. But Johnny's team has hit the Wisconsin roadways as part of a statewide AAU program.

I have never been a fan of this sporting youth traveling thing. Always shook my head incredulously at the hockey and soccer families who spend so many weekends in a Quality Inn somewhere. But John's coach has wisdom, and the travel demands have been sane.

In fact it has been great fun. A good way for my son to learn some guy things as he makes the tough transition from little boy to young man.

And it offers a chance to remember.

Some of the best times I have ever had have been on the road with teammates. There were Little League journeys to Otumwa, Iowa, and Joplin, Missouri, after we won the state championship. There were the high school trips to towns all over the state from Evansville to Sauk Prairie to New London.

And always we would sing.

There is a tribal urge when groups of men gather to raise their voices in song. Men sang on troop trains as they went off to two wars in Europe. They made music in the Civil War camps. And the oldest chants of all were sung beside our earliest campfires.

When I first took my high school football trips I was quickly made aware of the bus protocol. Seniors in the back, they led the singing. The songs were a mishmash of popular hits, oldies and ribald limericks set to music.

The highlight of the trip was when Coach Wilke would make his way from the front of the bus to the back and sing for us. The elder chief singing his song for the young braves.

As the adrenaline of the game wore off and the crazy songs

were sung, the bus would get quiet. Then, as we stared at the Wisconsin cornfields and towns slipping by in the night, a lone voice would start a ballad about a girl.

"I've got sunshine on a cloudy day," one guy would intone. And the other voices would join as one.

Older men sing the ballads too. Several years ago a busload of us made our way down to Chicago for a ball game. On our way home the songs began. The finale started slowly but built as it went, until the entire gang of lawyers, postal clerks, teachers, newspaper guys and bankers sang John Lennon's soulful lament at the top of their voices: "Oh, and this boy would be happy just to love you!"

Even the bus driver joined in.

It is quiet in the van now. The boys have played ball all day and they are tired. I stare out the window as we pass the Marshall exit.

Then I hear a voice begin a quiet song.

The other teammates pick up the melody. They sing the tune well, with the clear, clean sound that boys' voices possess the year before they deepen. I can hear my son's voice among them.

They are singing a ballad about a girl.

Regards,
John

August 1999

THE CANNES STORY

INTERIOR DAY An Air France jet somewhere over the Atlantic. A Midwestern couple is seated in business class eating dinner. JOHN is a faded middle-aged high school athlete desperately trying to keep a second chin at bay. He is seated next to his wife, the beautiful and charming DIANE.

DIANE: Boy, can you believe it? You and Mary Sweeney write a screenplay called *The Straight Story* and now we are going to the Cannes Film Festival.

Amazing! I sure hope my gown fits.

JOHN (mouth full): Gee, this French cheese is really good.

CUT TO

INT. DAY Cannes, France. Hotel room. The Savoy on the Riviera.

DIANE: I hardly have much jet lag at all! Let's go to the museum. Let's get a meal. Let's see if they have an art gallery!

JOHN (with binoculars): Sure. Or we could stroll the beach.

DIANE (snoring): Gzzmfft.

CUT TO

INT. EVENING Cannes, France. A cocktail party at a private club. In attendance are the key cast members including director DAVID

127

LYNCH, producer/writer/editor MARY SWEENEY, actors
RICHARD FARNSWORTH, SISSY SPACEK and HARRY
DEAN STANTON, as well as supporting actors and Madisonians
JOHN and KEVIN FARLEY, their recently widowed mother
MARY ANN and Mary Sweeney's charming sister PAT.

KEVIN FARLEY: Geez, Johnny can you believe we are here in
France?

JOHNNY FARLEY: This is tres cool. Is there something on my
shirt?

MARY ANN FARLEY: I just met Sissy Spacek. She is darling. And
just beautiful. I invited her to play bridge with my club if she ever
came to Madison.

PAT SWEENEY: I invited her to the Farmers' Market. (In a
whisper) I've heard she likes fresh produce.

CUT TO

EXT. EVENING Cannes, France. The red-carpeted stairs leading
up to the Palais du Festival, the theater in which *The Straight Story*
will be debuted.

DIANE: My God, look at all those photographers! I have to stay
calm or I am going to perspire. Look at all those stairs. Is my gown
wrinkled in back?

This is just wild. Where do we walk? Where do we look?

JOHN: Just follow David and Mary and smile. (Pauses.) I wish the
kids were here.

CUT TO

INT. THEATER The film is showing. The camera moves down the

aisle revealing the faces lit by the light of the film. We see the FARLEYS, PAT SWEENEY, and finally JOHN and DIANE. JOHN has a pleasantly stunned look on his face.

DIANE is dabbing her eyes with a tissue. The camera moves to the floor to reveal a pile of tissues at her feet.

CUT TO

EXT. NIGHT The stairs leading down from the theater. The music from the soundtrack plays out into the warm Riviera evening as a crowd stands below.

MARY ANN FARLEY comes up to JOHN, MARY SWEENEY, KEVIN and JOHNNY FARLEY and embraces each of them, a tear in her eye.

MARY ANN FARLEY: I am so proud of you kids. Richard Farnsworth was marvelous. David did such a wonderful job directing. The scenes of those country roads were beautiful. (She pauses, her eyes welling.) My Tom used to drive those roads. (Everyone reaches for a tissue.)

CUT TO

INT. EVENING Air France jet somewhere over the Atlantic. A tired JOHN and DIANE are settling down for the final hours of their return flight to the U.S. and home.

DIANE: This was all like a fairy tale. What an experience. We have so much to tell the kids. I can't wait to get the pictures developed. David and Mary sure did a wonderful job. And so did you, dear.

JOHN (reclining his seat to sleep): Thank you, Di.

DIANE: And honey—remember when we get home—it's trash day.

JOHN (eyes closed): Right.

FADE TO BLACK

October 1999

GUARANTEED COMPLIANT

Brian,

Now that the maple leaves have fallen and the nights are leaving shingle frost, it's time to take the end of the century more seriously. The press is creating all sorts of lists of interesting people and things of the past century that deserve all sorts of credit for being interesting people and things of the past century.

We have heard much about the Y2K issue. A variety of chip-driven machines are huddled in the corner whispering among themselves. They are talking about us. There is a rumor that they will start a rumble at the dance the instant the numbers roll over to 1/1/00.

We fear that, come the stroke of midnight, our lives will become non-compliant with the 21st century.

I feel compelled to create a list as well. This list has nothing to do with the past, however. This is a list about the future. Specifically, it's a list of The Things That Will Work in the First Second of the 21st Century. It's an important one, as my wife has been hoarding drinking water in empty milk cartons down in the basement since June.

GUARANTEED COMPLIANT

Please feel free to post it at home or at work.

The List of Things That Will Work in the First Second of the 21st Century

10. Roofs
9. Blankets
8. Flashlights

These first three Things That Will Work are all Y2K-compliant. Body Heat got votes here as well. Warmth and shelter are key if all systems of societal support crash, as they will do on what is traditionally one of the coldest nights of the year in Wisconsin and most places north of St. Louis. Sweaters, Gloves, and Rapidly Rubbing the Hands Together also received honorable mention given their effectiveness in the Y/1900 crisis.

7. Walking
6. Conversation
5. Playing euchre

Our panel of judges felt that if the light in your non-compliant digital refrigerator goes out, you can walk over to your neighbor's house, pull up a chair, separate the deck and complain about the light in the fridge. Standing on your front steps and hollering, "Hey, Wally, our fridge light went out!" also got votes here, as well as Wally bellowing back "The hell you say!"

4. Books
3. Candles
2. Firewood

According to experts, all books, other than e-books, are Y2K-compliant. Says Professor Lyle Delp of MIT, "We have turned pages of thousands of books trying to simulate Y2K conditions, and to date we have encountered very few problems." Candles are predicted to work well on January 1. Likewise, firewood, which provides both heat and light, looks to be a good bet come New Year's Eve, assuming that you do not try to light the cured oak with one of the new e-matches now available at fire.com.

And, finally, the No. 1 Thing That Will Work on the First Second of the 21st Century is:

1. Standing Upright

This is a surprise, as many thought sex was a lock for No. 1. But Standing Upright has always been a solid contender for the top honor.

My personal plans for the first seconds of the new century actually include Standing Upright. I hope to spend the last hours of the old century tucked away in our North Woods cabin, a fire glowing hot and warm in the fieldstone hearth. As the new century approaches, I am going to throw on a wool coat and walk out onto our frozen lake, stand upright, and look up to the stars so bright and clear in the northern sky. I will draw a deep breath and bid farewell to the 1900s, and welcome a new age of man.

However, if the stars above me begin to dim, I will run inside and begin amending the above list.

Regards,
John

November 1999

MY HEROES HAVE ALWAYS BEEN FIREMEN

Brian,

Wow what a crazy day in the neighborhood!

The guy next door, Lyle Delp? His garage caught on fire!

Lyle'd cleaned out his fireplace and stored the ashes in a paper bag next to his lawn mower gas. Then he and the little woman (that's what he, not me, calls her), they jump on the Harley with the sidecar and head to Steven's Point for the Sweet Adeline convention.

Anywhoooo...I'm outside ten minutes after they're gone and I see smoke comin' outta Lyle's garage. Quick as a blink I call 911 and they say the fire truck will be there pronto.

Then the damndest thing happens.

About four minutes later a cab pulls up and a fireman gets out.

Out of a taxi I say!

Not ten guys and a truck. Just one fireman. And he's got the coat and boots and big hat and all.

Now before I go further I gotta tell you that when I was a kid I thought firemen were heroes for sure. You'd walk by the neighborhood fire station and they'd let you inside and you'd stand and gawk at that big shiny truck. They'd sit out there on a chair in the sun and talk to you and boy they were impressive fellas.

I remember when we lost a few of those men back in the 'sixties. It was a sad day. The saddest.

So anyhow he walks up to me and asks if he can use my garden hose and I say "Anything, sir!" Then quick and smart he traipses around the house, gets my hose and starts laying down water on the fire. While he's doin' it we start talkin'.

"So why the taxi? And only one man responding to the call?" I ask, trying to use a little fire department lingo.

The fireman gets a kinda unhappy look on his face and says, "Well ordinarily we would have responded with about ten fire fighters and a truck but things have been a little...ah, unusual, at the fire department these days."

I go, "So I've noticed. So where's your truck and fellow firefighters?"

"Well, the fire truck, and an ambulance and four of the firefighters from our station responded to a paramedic call. A nine year old with prickly heat." He says.

"Geez," I says, "I can see the ambulance, but why do you need a fire truck for a prickly heat call?"

"Policy." He explains while he's smoothly and professionally working the fire down with my green hose.

"OK," I says. "That explains the truck I guess, but what about the other firefighters?"

He's got the fire under control now. He's a real pro.

"Well two men from our station have been suspended for

suspicion of cocaine use." He winces when he says this.

I tell him that I used to know a fella who had a taste for that stuff. He was in a Dave Clark Five tribute band that hit it big for about six months. After he cleaned up he told me that using cocaine was God's way of tellin' you that you have too much money and too much time on your hands.

"Could be," he says. Then he tells me two of the other firefighters have a business on the side and they called in sick because it's the busy season for their other jobs.

"Must be nice. That leaves one more fire firefighter." I say.

"At a union meeting." he says. "The union has some problems with the Chief. Lot of the members think she's incompetent."

"Could be," I say, "but at least she's not a felon."

By this time he had saved Lyle's garage from complete destruction.

He rolls up my hose and puts it back in its place. On the way back to the front yard he got my cat out of a tree. I shake his hand and thank him.

He looks at me and says, "I became a Madison fireman not for the pension or the lifestyle or to set up a side business or to tell people how hard my job was or to be a party boy or to bitch about the chief at union meetings." He pauses. "I became a firefighter because I wanted to help people. Maybe even be a hero sometime."

Then he looks me in the eye and says, "If someone was in that garage, I would have gone in and got them out."

I told him I thought he was a hero.

In fact, I'd like to tell you the name of this Madison firefighter. But the city, and the union, wouldn't release it.

Regards,
John

June 2000

ANGELS IN THE OUTFIELD

Brian,

The Fourth of July is a fun holiday.

When I was young it meant Westmoreland Park and an all-day celebration. The centerpiece of the festivities prior to the fireworks was a softball game.

Madison softball was big in the '60s. The *State Journal* and *Capital Times* covered the exploits of fireballing Willie Taylor and others with big headlines, not the agate type that such exploits have been relegated to these days.

The featured contest on the Fourth at Westmoreland was an annual neighborhood grudge match; Glenway Liquor versus Bridge Lounge. This was a game between Madison guys who had been playing together and against each other for years.

Glenway Liquor consisted mostly of Edgewood alums (my dad included); guys who had played for the legendary Earl Wilke during the Crusaders' mid-40s reign of victories and undefeated seasons. The Bridge Lounge guys were stellar athletes too; Edgewood, Central and West High grads of the same vintage.

The games were always fun. The hollow that is the Westmoreland diamond made for a natural amphitheater. This was the era of big families and it seemed like each player had sired eight kids. The hill would be filled with family members, wives and kids, watching and cheering. After the game, always hotly contested, the two teams and their families would make their way to the beer tent and enjoy the Fourth of July and the fireworks.

Schim Elliott played for Bridge Lounge. His brother Howie was on the team too. Schim occupied the hot box, third base, a position in softball that requires no small amount of courage. The base paths in softball are not as long as those in regulation baseball. A cagey, courageous third baseman will sneak up the line to take away the bunt, placing himself at risk of a wicked line drive. Schim did that.

Bill Rock, aka "Doc," played for Glenway Liquor. Bill's game was not quite the caliber of Schim's. Bill Crowley, another physician and the colorful manager of the Glenway Liquor squad, would usually insert Doc Rock into right field late in the game.

Schim Elliott and Doc Rock recently crossed paths. But it was not on the Fourth of July.

Several years ago Schim Elliott developed cancer. The initial diagnosis was grave. But due to good care and pure pluck (the same toughness he showed at third base), Schim proved the doctors wrong. He muscled the cancer for years; going to daily Mass, playing a little golf, watching his granddaughter play basketball.

This spring things took a turn. Elliott's family called Doc Rock. A leader in the local hospice care movement, Doc has been helping Madison folks in their last days for quite a while now.

Doc Rock visited Schim Elliott's bedside and had the conversation that he has had with so many people in Madison. The conversation that many doctors can't seem to handle.

The two talked for hours. Doc whispering in his ear, Schim slipping in and out. Doc telling Schim it was OK to go.

Then Doc told Schim a story. He told Schim about a game they had going out there. All the guys from Glenway Liquor and Bridge Lounge who had passed on. The guys who had played those games on the Fourth of July? They were waiting for him.

Waiting on the field at Westmoreland.

And then Doc went over the lineup with Schim.

There's the Glenway boys, Schim. Dick Riesen and Ralph Riley, playing catch with those small leather pillows they call gloves. Watch speedy Donnie Schaeffer loping in center field. There's Doc Crowley barking at the guys. And pitchers Jack King and Shortie Ross are warming up on the sideline.

Over there are the guys from the Bridge Lounge squad, Schim. Volkmann, Mader, and Ol' Rag Arm, Donnie Schmelzer.

With Doc Rock helping him, Schim Elliott passed away.

We will celebrate the Fourth again this year. The red, white and blue crepe will hang from the bikes in the parade. Blankets will be spread on the ground. Fire will light the sky. And on the Westmoreland softball field, some of us will see the ghosts of Glenway Liquor and Bridge Lounge, laughing, playing and sliding hard into second.

Doc Rock will probably enjoy the Fourth too. Unless, of course, he is called to someone's bedside.

After all, though Bill Rock played a little right field for Glenway Liquor, he is not yet a ghost.

But surely, he is a saint.

Regards,
John

July 2000

A TAP ON THE HORN

Brian,

When you live in a city the size of Madison, you are more often reminded not of how big our city is, but how small we are. We are separated by a mere six degrees from knowing everyone in the world, but in Madison that connection is often reduced to two.

Take Mike, for example. Nice guy. Knew him when he was in

grade school at Blessed Sacrament on the near west side. A sweet kid and talented basketball player. Classic jump shot and remarkable composure for an eighth grader.

Upon my return to Madison after nearly a decade in Chicago I would happen upon Mike, now a grown family man, jogging in the Arboretum or standing in line at Michael's Frozen Custard. We would nod, smile and chat a bit.

Mike has a touch of the entrepreneur in him. He opened a cycle and ski shop on Monroe Street before moving it to the bustling corner on Mineral Point across from the Village Bar and the picturesque first tee of Glenway Golf Course. You can grab a coffee at his place in the morning.

So it was with a cold shudder that I read the story about the young West High student who died after attending a rave at the Barrymore last month. His name was Brett, and he bore Mike's last name. His picture confirmed my fear; he looked just like his dad when he was that age.

A week after Brett's passing I stopped in to see Mike. He works alone at his shop most days. He was waiting on an older couple who were mulling over a pair of bicycle pants. He caught my eye but did not flash the usual friendly smile; an act hard to come by these days.

He walked over. I asked him how he was doing, and he told me things were hard. As hard as things can be. We talked for a few minutes about the investigation into his son's death and the rough days he was living through before he had to get back to his customers. I left, but my thoughts have stayed with Mike.

And others.

There have been too many of these stories in the last few years.

The Farley family buried their talented son Chris just a few years ago.

A Middleton family lost their son last year and now wage a courageous battle to find and prosecute the drug dealer whose street business cost them their child's life.

And, like many, I struggle with what to do and say to them. I don't have the words.

But I did hear some three Decembers ago.

It was at Chris Farley's funeral. Two priests spoke. One was young and offered little wisdom to my mind. But then a tough old Jesuit priest from Chicago walked to the pulpit. He had been Chris' counselor in Chicago.

This man addressed his remarks directly to Chris' parents, brothers and sisters. It was to them alone that he spoke, though the church was full.

He told them that he personally struggled with Chris' death. He observed that if you are a believer in any type of God it challenges your faith. You ask yourself, "Where was God that night as Chris, your son and brother, lay dying?"

The Jesuit, a strong and holy man, told the family that he had prayed long and hard on that question.

Then he looked at the Farleys and told them that he had found the answer.

"Your son Chris was not alone that night. God was right there with him."

As for Mike, I plan to buy some cross country gear from him this fall.

A small way to show I care.

But I also had a notion of how folks in a small town could show a neighbor that they are thinking about him and his family as they round the curve on their way to work.

When you drive by the corner of Mineral Point and Glenway, tap your horn.

Sure, it will feel hokey the first time, and may mess with a few backswings, but it takes only a second, and Mike would be sure to hear it.

A TAP ON THE HORN

Even if you never met him, or his son, it's a small town way to let a neighbor know that your thoughts are with him.
And that he too, is not alone.

Regards,
John

November 2000

LESSONS OF THE FALL

Brian,

The mist rises early in the morning and hangs in the boughs of the white pines.

The battle for the lake's surface continued overnight. The ice is slowly defeating the open water. This is the timeless event we watch up north this time of year.

Over at the good neighbors' place, Curt and Carolyn Parker are hunkered down for winter. Curt, the handiest man in the world, just set new steps leading to their cabin. He got them done before the ground froze. They offer sure footing as I walk to their door.

The Parkers are their usual hospitable selves. Carolyn, a strong, smart woman, displays an intricate pine needle basket she is weaving.

"Something to do while we watch to see who's going to be

president." She motions to the small television set. "Can you believe this?"

"Never seen anything like it," Curt echoes.

Carolyn chuckles and corrects him. "Yes we have."

They jog my memory. Carolyn ran for the Vilas County Board a few years back. She was tired of the unenlightened views of the sitting members of that body. She felt that that they were slowly developing the beauty out of one of Wisconsin's most beautiful counties. So she decided to do something about it.

Carolyn Parker campaigned door to door, shaking as many hands as she could. Curt, a patriot of the first order as a 20-year Navy man, acted as her campaign manager. He helped print the flyers and yard signs. He also offered his wife advice on the realities of local politics in the North Woods.

Carolyn's opponent was a woman who thought Lady Bird Johnson was wrong to discourage Americans from throwing trash out of our car windows. Carolyn ran as an unabashed friend of the environment.

The voters of Vilas County, Wisconsin had a clear choice. They spoke. On election night Carolyn Parker won by one vote. 116 to 115. Ms. Parker's opponent requested a hand recount of the stylus-punched ballots.

Did Carolyn oppose the request?

"No. I thought it was the logical thing to do. Machines make mistakes," she says, while looking out at the partially frozen lake. A fire burns in the wood stove.

Curt remembers. "The county clerk came and put all the ballots in a metal lock box and off we went. They said they'd do the recount in an office at the courthouse."

What kind of ballots?

"The kind with chads," they both laugh.

"I wasn't there for all that. I had to work," recalls Carolyn. She was employed as a substitute teacher.

Curt attended as a vigilant observer. "The clerk's secretary was a pal of Carolyn's opponent, if you know what I mean."

Curt details the drama.

"They had three old ladies at a table with the county secretary. The secretary explained the process to them. The clerk himself kept running in and out of the room." Curt continued. "The secretary would grab a ballot and jab a pencil at it, damn near knocking a chad out. I said, 'Hey, I don't think you're supposed to handle those things that way. Treat those ballots with respect.' She pretty much ignored me. All the while she's chatting with Carolyn's opponent."

The recount took two and a half hours. The county secretary and clerk declared a tie.

Curt was not happy.

"I told the county clerk that we were going to protest the recount. He ran out of the room." Out of the room? "Yeah, he got on the phone to Madison and the state Elections Board. I think he was a little flustered."

What was Carolyn's reaction to democracy at work?

"I was surprised at how much I didn't know about politics," Carolyn laughed. "We were both a little disappointed that things were so subjective."

What did Curt learn?

"You gotta be on your toes."

And how did things get resolved?

"The clerk goes into the sheriff's office and comes back with a hat," says Curt with a laugh.

A hat?

"Yeah, they decided to draw the winner out of a hat. It belonged to a sheriff's deputy. It was a brownish green. Had a black bill. I told them I didn't approve, but they did it anyway. I never saw them write the names on the slips or anything."

Kind of suspenseful?

"Yup. And damn if they didn't draw Carolyn's name."

Ms. Carolyn Parker, American, served two terms on the Vilas County Board.

The next morning I awake to see that our lake is completely frozen. It is a strange process, this thing that happens on our lake in late fall, but it always seems to get done.

Regards,
John

January 2001

UNCLE DING

Brian,

Everyone has an Uncle Ding.

He's the eternally effervescent relative who snaps four hundred pictures at every family gathering. The one who emails you an endless string of corny jokes. The guy who sends an annual blizzard of newspaper clippings that just might be interesting to you, with a handwritten scribble that states, "Thought this might be interesting to you."

The quaint thing about my Uncle Ding is that he isn't my uncle. He is my mother's cousin. If he wasn't such a nice guy, Ding would be described as a shirttail relative. But he has been crowned with the avuncular title by everyone in our family because he acts like one to all of us.

He remembers birthdays.

He knows the names of kids who aren't his grandchildren.

He hugs you when he sees you.

That's Uncle Ding for you.

Even though he is not the brother of either my mother or my father, everyone in our family likes the fact that Ding is our uncle.

Given my mother's family history, this affection for Ding is understandable. Both he and my mother had it tough as children. My mother was orphaned at the age of 11. Ding's father died at a very young age. My mother and her few Chicago cousins cling to each other because there are so very few of them. They are their only family.

A few months ago I got a call from Mom asking me to keep Ding in my thoughts. He was not doing well. Now 66 years old, Ding has struggled with a chronic heart condition for more than 20 years. For the last 10 years, he has had to wear a defibrillator, an implanted device that shocks the heart into action when it stops. This thing gives your thumper a serious shot. A defibrillator is to a pacemaker as a car battery is to a Ray-O-Vac AAA.

These staggering jolts have kept Ding alive. It must be a very tough thing to be aware of every beat of your heart for over two decades.

This Christmas, after an unsuccessful procedure at the Mayo Clinic to rewire the electric impulses that operated his heart, Ding was hospitalized. We suspected things were grave when they did not send him home for the holidays. A few days later Mom called in tears and told me that Ding was dying. The medical report was filled with frightening terms like "cardiomyopathy" and "global enlargement."

Then, a day later, I got another call. Mom again. In an excited voice, she announced, "Johnny, you are not going to believe this, but Ding got a new heart! And he's doing great!"

We are nonchalant about transplants these days. Especially with the wonder they perform right here in Madison. But when it is someone you know who is pulled from the brink, you are stunned.

It is a true, unadulterated miracle.

I talked to Ding today. He is home and doing great. There are no signs of rejection. He reports that he is driving Dar, his long-suffering wife, pleasantly nuts, as we all knew he would.

Ding told me that he has very little memory of the hours prior to his resurrection. He was only at the top of the transplant list for a few days. He knows that he was open and on the operating table while the Lear jet, with a medical team of four and his new heart, was still in the air.

Next week Ding starts driving. The doctor expects him to be mowing the lawn this April. They are also letting him eat anything he wants for a while, before he returns to the more stringent dietary menu he has followed so well for so long.

"I am going to have a Braunschweiger and onion on Rosen's rye," Ding declared. "But just one."

Ding has not met the family of his donor. There are confidentiality procedures that the hospital imposes. The donor's family can reach out to the recipient if they care to make contact.

Right now, Ding does not know whose heart beats in his chest. No notion of gender, race or occupation. But he does know one thing: it came from Ohio.

"I pray for a family in Ohio every day," Ding says. "You pray for them too, OK?"

I tell Uncle Ding that I will.

And then he says, "And tell everyone in Madison that I used to love them with all of my Chicago heart, and now I love them with all of my Ohio heart."

That's my Uncle Ding for you.

Regards,
John

March 2001

ROBIN'S NEST

Brian,

For the last several springs a mom robin has chosen to make her nest above a porch light just to the right of our front door. In early spring, while it is still cold, she flutters madly about with small wisps of grass until her nest is made.

Shortly thereafter you can peek over the edge of her construction effort to spy baby robins chirping blindly. I assume Ma and Pa Robin prefer the warmth provided by the light and the shelter from spring winds that the porch provides.

The perch also offers haven from the neighborhood cats, who sit in predatory stillness in the driveway and stare up at the nest, waiting for a single misstep by the robin family.

The baby birds grow quickly. By late spring they have flown away. The nest is vacated.

It all happens so fast.

This will be a special spring around our household. One of our own is perched on the edge of the nest. Our eldest, daughter Kate, graduates from high school.

This too, has happened so quickly.

Just how we got from the first day of kindergarten at Leopold Elementary to the last days at Edgewood High School is a blink. It is not possible to recount it all in real time. What you are left with is lessons, impressions, memories and a host of new friendships you never anticipated.

When you begin a family you are very conscious of what you must teach your children.

Don't put that in your mouth.

Don't cross that street.

Don't worry, everything will work out.

But now as our circle of parents and families prepare to send off this year's flock of newly minted adults, I am struck not by what we have taught my daughter. Instead I am most thoughtful of what she, her friends, and their families have given us.

Kate and her friends have taught me about the glories of CD burning and the freedom of downloadable music.

They have taught me about instant messaging.

They have taught me that this generation of boys have remarkably large feet.

I have also learned, through observation, the migratory patterns of teens.

Like friendly grackles finding a tree or phone line, they assemble in the early evening and take flight. They then flutter down to settle en masse in a chosen basement to watch the latest Adam Sandler epic or horror flick. Suddenly on a whim, phone call, opinion, or simple boredom, they all take flight, leaving as quickly as they arrived, looking to descend on another basement in another house. As much as I will miss my daughter when she heads off to college, I also will miss her friends. They have become a joyful constant in our household.

I will miss Lizzy freely perusing our cupboard for snacks while she fires off one incredibly witty comment after another.

I will miss the flurry of activity and pictures before Homecoming and Prom.

I will miss Kathryn's keen analytical skills, total recall and shy smile.

I will miss the benign conspiracy and good counsel from the other parents.

I will miss game night—all of them.

I will miss Jason and B actually having a real conversation with the male parental upstairs while the rest of the gang is downstairs.

I will miss Sara's smile, Becky's grin and Kelly's energetic entrances.

I will miss all the guys like Brad, Brice, Brian and Clint who looked me in the eye, shook my hand and said, "Hi Mr. Roach."

I will miss less so the guys who stared at the floor and said nothing.

Most of all I will miss the large pile of tennis shoes in our front hallway. This is my favorite sign that the herd has assembled at our house. It is accompanied by the corresponding laughter and shrieks rising up from the basement and the dutiful "Hi Mr. Roach" that greets me when I make my regularly scheduled walk through the sprawled throng to make sure that all is well and right on the bottom floor.

I will miss all of this. And all of them.

When they play the graduation march, and the birds on the edge of the nest make their way down the aisle, I will quietly thank them. They have made me a happier human and a better dad. Better prepared for the odyssey of Kate's younger sister and brother and their friends who, as I write and smile, are already laughing in our basement and raiding our cupboard.

Stay in touch.

Come visit at Thanksgiving break.

Leave your tennis shoes in the front hall, just inside the door from our front porch light.

The one with the robin's nest on it.

Regards,
John

April 2001

HE WON'T BITE

Brian,

There are days when you read the newspaper and just shake your head.

Like the story out of Dodgeville where a couple is suing their neighbor for $50,000 for shooting their dog. The shooter claims the dog was regularly harassing his children.

A woman in Racine is taking legal action against a police officer for dispatching her cute little Rottweiler.

While these dog owners were filing suit, a San Francisco family was burying their grown daughter who was mauled to death at her apartment door by the neighbor's mutts.

Huge numbers of people are dashed to the emergency room every day with dog bites.

Most of them are children. The lucky ones are able to survive with a mild case of disfiguring wounds. In that respect, dogs are right up there with handguns.

The words these hapless kids and their parents most likely heard before their flesh was bloodily rent asunder was that soothing, dopey mantra that all dog owners intone at one time or another: "Don't worry. He won't bite."

Of course they are wrong. Dogs bite. Along with soiling your lawn, it's what they do. What dog owners mean when they smile and utter those words is, really, "Don't worry. He won't bite me."

I know some dogs are cute and smart and charming. Some are, in fact, man's best friend. They provide company and security for many of us who need it. They even use dogs on TV commercials along with baby humans to create an instant sense of endearment.

But as a former jogger and current cyclist, I am regularly stunned by the gross assumptions made by many dog owners. They assume that I am unbothered by their leashless pooch as it dashes in front of my bike. They assume that I am at ease as their dog dashes after me.

They assume that I am relaxed as their pooch sloppily noses my crotch.

They are wrong. I am bothered by it. I view an unleashed dog as a gun out of a holster.

And here is the rub. For all of their smiles and genial excuses for the pooch's behavior, I think that dog owners who impose their pets on others knowingly engage in a form of social aggression. Dogs act as a physical extension of the owner. For whatever reason, some people use their canines to make other humans uncomfortable. They get away with it because they smile while it happens.

As if it is charming when King sticks his nose in your crotch.

Like these folks would smile if I stuck my nose in their crotch.

As for the Dodgeville case, I have a personal perspective. We had neighbors at our former house who owned a mean German Shepherd. They regularly let it out of their house unleashed. More than once it rushed our three children, who were all under the age of seven at the time. The dog's hackles would be raised, its teeth bared. We would hear the screams that "the dog was loose" and run to collect our little ones. We tried talking to the owners but they failed to leash the dog consistently. Several neighbors called the police. Still the issue remained unresolved.

I must admit that if I had owned a gun, I would have shot that animal in an instant.

Not because I hate dogs, but because I love my offspring and view it as my job to protect them.

I do not think, however, that I would have done the same thing with the German Shepherd's body as the guy in Dodgeville did with the animal that he killed.

But I can almost understand.

He threw it off a cliff. I think he was trying to make a statement.

The attorney for the bereaved dogless couple claims this about his legal action: "This case is about human rights and a creature that is part of a human family."

Of course, you could say the same thing about children.

Regards,
John

June 2001

ACROSS THE SEA TO IRELAND

Brian,

There is a favorite Irish ballad called *Galway Bay* that poses a question in its first verse. It asks, "Have you ever been across the sea to Ireland?"

I have never been able to answer that question in the affirmative. Until last month.

In honor of their 50th wedding anniversary, John and Mary Gene Roach flew all six of their adult children and themselves across the Atlantic to visit the land that holds our roots. Our forefathers and -mothers, in the 1800s, left Ireland for Madison, opting to consume too much cheese rather than too many potatoes.

Here now is a moment-by-moment chronicle of events.

Depart Chicago with parents and hero travel agent sister and trip planner Mary Beth on Virgin Atlantic. Irony of parents flying Virgin to celebrate wedding anniversary is not lost on anyone. Folks fly first class. Forefathers traveled to America in steerage, but Mom and Dad returning in style.

Rendezvous in Limerick with siblings who flew Aer Lingus. Celebrate in hotel restaurant with Harp and Guinness. Marvel at what we pulled off: dodged major family events, gained blessing of spouses and children, met halfway around the world to celebrate parents' marriage.

Night One. 10 p.m. Roommate and brother Dan explains he needs white noise of small fan to sleep. Fine. Brother plugs in fan without European electrical adapter. Steps into washroom. Fan begins to make strange noise. Shoots a ball of flame across room. Emits cloud of acrid smoke. Brother Dan comes out of bathroom. Asks, "Where did all this smoke come from?"

10:15 p.m. Brother Dan runs out to purchase new fan. Only store open? Roches (original spelling of our name) Department Store. Ancestors help Dan sleep.

Day Two. Drive on left side of road to Galway Resort and Country Club. Play golf with brothers. Must convert metric to yards to determine distance to pin. To my dismay and their delight I suffer humiliating loss to brothers Jim and Dan. Consider return to America, but am too charmed by literally watching the sun go down on Galway Bay.

Night Two. Roaches descend on resort pub. Sister Sue begins to dance and sing in loud operatic voice. Crowd of Irish celebrants, including two first communions and one wedding reception, find Yank girl amusing.

Day Three. More golf. Brother Dan missing at first tee. Locked in bathroom wearing only towel. Begins having claustrophobic attack. Bangs on walls to get attention of maids. Fan works fine.

Day Four. Travel agent Mary Beth wants everyone to go on a tour of local sites. Brother Bob, official trip videotapist, agrees to drive. I play golf alone in rain and work on metric math. Later have coffee in lobby and think to self, "That desk manager looks like one of the Madison Sweeneys." Ask fellow his name. "Liam," he smiles, "Liam Sweeney."

Night. Roach kids make way into downtown Galway for pizza. Visit pub. Sister Sue dances and sings in operatic voice, again electrifying the crowd. Go outside and come upon two young women street singers. Sing with Brother Jim and the Irish girls. Family joins. Irish songs at midnight.

Day Five. Go to Mother's Day Mass in small town of Orenmore. Long time since all kids have been at Mass with Mom and Dad. Reluctant Brother Bob silent during Mass. Then, priest intones, "The Mass is ended, go in Peace." Brother Bob says at top of voice, "Thanks be to God!" Siblings can't stop laughing.

Night. Last night in Galway. Make way to thatched roof pub, McDonoughs. Locals love having season's first Americans arrive. Dad buys the pub a round. This inspires a local, Dennis Mackey, whose brother lives in Eau Claire, to run out to car and bring in banjo. He tunes, slurps down a Guinness, wipes the foam from his grizzle and begins to play. We sing for three hours. First time Mom is in a bar past midnight since VJ Day.

Day Six. Leave for Killarney. Ride with Mom and Dad. Mom loves farmhouses. Dad loves stone fences. "The Irish have lifted a lot of stones!"

Day Seven. Killarney. Brothers golf at Mahoney's Point. Mother and sisters in shopping frenzy. Crisis: how to fit all gifts in bags.

Day Eight. Last day in Ireland. Family dinner. We toast our parents.

Day Nine. Return home to loved ones, tired and happy. Final irony: went to discover ancestral roots but instead rediscovered our own family for a week.

Happy anniversary, Mom and Dad.

Regards,
John

July 2001

2002

SHOVEL, ANYONE?

Whilst watching news of the war on Madison's sundry cable stations, I have been struck by how much information we are being asked to absorb when all we really want to know is whether some lucky Marine from Fayetteville, Louisiana, has succeeded in shooting Mr. Bin Laden in the head.

Even as we inquire as to the fate of a place where women have to wear dirty sheets over their heads while being subjected to the occasional caning, we are also being given real-time stock quotes, the primetime lineup for the evening, last night's Memphis Grizzlies rebounding stats, a graphic of that snowstorm over the Rockies and a web address where we can get even more information.

You may think you are slouching on your couch, but you are actually being multitasked.

This is not just a television phenomenon.

Take a look at your average teen these days. They don't come home from school and plop on the sofa with a bag of Fritos and numbly stare at *American Bandstand* for an hour, as was done in a previous era. No sireee. Today they unshoulder that physical proof of multitasking, their 78-pound bookbag, drop it in the middle of the hallway, prance immediately to the computer to go online, begin to instant message 70 friends even as they commence writing that term paper, downloading that web picture, dialing a friend on the phone, getting dressed for practice and zapping their dinner of Ramen noodles.

The now familiar jingle of the next instant message popping onto a computer screen is the multitasking tune to which the Millennial Generation dances.

Attention deficit is no longer a developmental problem, it's a personal asset. And it ain't just kids.

Technology has given all of us the freedom to listen to voicemail while we answer email while we shuffle those low-tech Post-It notes on our desks while we answer a question from a cubicle colleague who is doing the same thing while talking to us.

This is not all bad. We are a much more productive society because of multitasking. Each of us is now lucky enough to do the work that took three or four people to accomplish just a generation ago. Rows of deskbound secretaries took hours to type what we now handle alone, in one second, by clicking the Forward icon.

But what is multitaskification doing to our species?

Granted, it is interesting that we can fire up so many synapses in our brains and run them concurrently, but just because we can do it does not mean it is swell. I can rev the engine of my car, play the radio and work the wipers for five hours straight, but that doesn't mean it is good for the sedan.

Indeed, there are times that I am so jazzed on multitasking that I have to stop and remember to breathe.

And then, for that moment, I imagine something novel. A single task.

Like those days long ago when I would stand outside and just rake leaves. One task. Leaf raking. Nothing more.

Or when I would step into the cold of a snowy evening with nothing but me, a shovel and a driveway in need of clearing. Again, one task.

Or when, as a youth, I would stand on the back of a wagon and grab the hay bale as it came off the conveyer and swing it onto the stack. The only multitasking I would do was wipe my brow between bales.

That's the thing about multitasking. You are doing a lot but you are not sweating. How can it be work if you are not sweating?

Multitasking has changed our physiology in a different way. Our blood holds more caffeine than it did a generation ago. Is it any wonder that Starbucks and its nerve-jangling java has blossomed in the age of hyper work? We need that buzz to task even faster and keep up with the daily tech evolutions that sometimes make us wonder if the machines are working for us or if we, like those poor goofs in Kubrick's 2001 spaceship, are working for them.

The best proof of that is simple. Do you ever see anyone break into a smile when their cell phone rings? Hell no, it's the multitask scowl that breaks over their face and the faces of most everyone with them. It's the irritating tug on the psychological sleeve from the silicon supervisor that won't leave you alone.

And finally, there is the dread fear that at the end of our lives, all of this work will have come to naught. That our efficient work only made for more work.

And that, for all the many tasks we accomplished, we made the mistake of confusing activity with achievement.

January 2002

IN PERFECT HARMONY

I am tooling east on I-94, making one of the many treks to Beer Town that my day job requires. In the car's six-disc CD player resides a smattering of albums and artists.

A favorite Van Morrison live performance from 1976 entitled *Too Late to Stop Now*.

A couple of lush Sinatra discs that get better every time they spin.

David Byrne's live tour de force, *Stop Making Sense*, with his surprisingly prescient *Life During Wartime*.

And of course, Marvin Gaye's seminal *What's Goin' On?*

An eclectic mix of classics that complement most every mood. Historically, The Three Tenors have occupied the final slot, adding energy and a touch of culture. I can never resist, as I drive and warble, attempting to hit Pavarotti's high note in *Nessun Dorma*. Unlike the portly and manic genius, I must slip into cheap, tinny falsetto to do the job.

But Luciano and his compadres have now been benched for the one disc that calls to me the loudest. It is distinctive for two reasons.

It was a gift.

And it is downloaded contraband.

It all started with daughter Maggie. While on a long drive north she popped in a selection that she had downloaded and burned. She thought I might like it.

She was right. But what I liked more were the sensibilities that she exposed through her musical selections. She unknowingly provided a snapshot of herself, and secondarily, her view of her dad's tastes.

Her mix was killer. After seeing my enthusiastic response, son JT took things one step further. "Dad, I'm gonna burn a disc just for you. I know what you like."

A generation ago, the generation gap was a very real thing. Youthful hair, clothes and level of patriotism and religious diligence were often in direct conflict with those of the folks.

That conflict is less sharp these days. At times there seems to be none at all. Ironically, the whole family can buy clothes at The Gap, a name first coined when there really was one.

A few days later, JT presented me with the disc that he had created. He smiled and said, "Don't worry, Dad, no hip-hop." (OK, so there is a little bit of a gap.)

I swapped The Tenors for my son's mix and frankly forgot about it for a few days. Then one evening, after a mind-numbing series of meetings, I slumped into my car and headed home from Milwaukee. A disc whirred, but it served as a mere background track to the bevy of calls that had to be returned in transit.

Just as the final call ended, the disc changed.

Out of nowhere, a machine gun riff fired and my eyebrows lifted. I realized I was hearing my son's gift for the first time.

What followed was a joyous thing.

Although I had heard snippets of these artists drifting over the airwaves on the kid-mandated Z104, this was the first time I listened closely to blink-182, Matchbox 20, the Goo Goo Dolls, Ben Folds Five, Uncle Kracker and SR-71. Each cut was better than the one before it. Fresh, fun, touching, stunning.

I have often remarked in know-it-all dinner conversation that, although Ronald Reagan may deserve some recognition, it was rock 'n' roll that really led to the fall of the Berlin Wall. After all, the youthful cry of rock is pretty much what freedom sounds like.

Those Eastern Europeans knew liberty when they heard it. Even Gorby and Yeltsin tapped their feet at the end. I am hearing the same tune now.

In the tracks and lyrics of my son's musical gift lay the joy, insecurity, pathos and passion that the world offers when it is not dusty and predictable, but new and promising.

The headlights are on and only the dash lights the interior. Ten miles ago I was tired. Now I am bobbing my head like Wayne and Garth.

At the end of the day, in the middle of my life, alone in my car, my son is singing his songs to me.

March 2002

THE WHATCHAMACALLIT MONOLOGUES

It is not quite clear how Lyle came up with the idea for the Grant County Cribbage Association fundraiser. Some said it was because his wife's younger sister, the one who's been studying feminist anthropology for the last two decades, went to the you-know-what Monologues in Madison. She mentioned it to Lyle after he'd had three brandy Manhattans and it just kinda took off from there.

At any rate, Lyle told all the guys that there was a charity gathering at the Tim Top Tap on Tuesday night to support local cribbage endeavors. When the group ambled in there were four chairs up on the stage where the polka bands usually play. Lyle, DuWayne, Carl and Carl's goofy cousin Buck were sitting in them.

"OK then, settle down," Lyle hollered. "We're here tonight to talk about our...well...male member for charity."

"What?" DuWayne yelped. "I thought we was talking about cribbage!"

Lyle shook his head. "Nope. We're gonna talk about our male member."

"All our cribbage club members are male." Carl was quick to point out. "The wives play hearts."

Lyle took a deep breath. "No, we are going to talk about how we feel about our...uh...er..." Lyle looked up at the ceiling for a moment and flashed on the notion that he might have to leave town. "What I'm tryin' to say is that this is the Penis Monologues."

The audience stared slack-jawed at Lyle. O'Hearn the farmer crossed himself, threw down his drink and looked toward the door. Several of the fellas unconsciously adjusted themselves.

Then cousin Buck, who has a plate in his head piped up. "I don't know about mine, but you should see my brother's."

DuWayne cut him off. "We really don't need to talk about..."

But Buck was on a roll. "...Anna a buddy a mine at the shop was in the Packers locker room once and he told me..."

By now DuWayne had heard enough. "Carl, shut yer goofy cousin's trap.

Lyle, just what is going on here?"

Lyle drew a deep breath. "My wife's sister says it's good to talk about yer privates. It's liberating."

"When I'm drinking beer I have to go into the Gentlemen's Room 'bout every twenty minutes to liberate mine." Buck grinned. "An' if I'm wearin' a snowmobile suit I gotta leave some extra time to locate it." This got a chuckle out of everyone and took some pressure off of Lyle.

Suddenly, out of nowhere, Carl blurted, "I got mine caught in my zipper when I was ten."

Everyone in the crowd winced.

"My dad had to use Ivory soap to fix it...that zipper, that is."

The crowd drew a collective sigh of relief. O'Hearn hurriedly ordered another pitcher and a shot of VO.

"I fell through the ice once and didn't see mine for a week," someone hollered from the back. This time the laughter was louder.

Lyle, in a professorial tone, offered a tidbit he had read on the subject. "That fella Presley called his Little Elvis."

"My ma called it a talleywhacker," offered the strangely talkative Carl.

"Hey," chimed Buck, "I gotta muskie lure called a Talley Whacker. Now that must mean something, eh?" Buck looked at Lyle thoughtfully for keen analysis. Lyle shrugged.

And then the names started flying.

"Johnson." "Willie." "Whatchamacallit." "Wedding tackle." "Thingy."

Finally the flurry died. There was a moment of meditative silence before Carl uttered the words that would make Grant County Cribbage Club history.

"My wife calls mine Scout."

Everyone studied their feet at this detail, knowing full well they would never look at Carl's wife in the same way again.

Lyle lunged at this awkward moment to extricate himself from the mess that three strong Manhattans and his crazy sister-in-law had gotten him into.

"Ok. Well then, thank you everyone for coming to the fundraiser. Let's play some cards."

Lyle then turned to Carl. "Your deal...Scout."

April 2002

▬

PERFECT AND STILL GROWING

I call it "the chair" because it is the piece of furniture around which our little cabin was built. It is the green leather thing that was perfectly constructed for reading a good book while listening to Billie Holiday, Dianna Krall or Neil Young as the voices of the kids, or the peepers in the bay, or the snort of a doe make their way to the ears.

I say that the cabin was built around "the chair." It's true.

Over 10 years ago, when we made the leap to build our own place on the lake where our family has found solitude for over 30 years, I walked the lot with our affable builder. Not being one who is deft with plots and plans, I asked Scott, "So where will we put the place?" He showed me in general terms where the cabin would be sited on the land.

I pressed him, "So where will the living room be?" He paced it off.

I pushed further. "So where will my reading chair be?" Walking around in the maples, birches and spruce, he showed me roughly where the chair would sit. "The fieldstone fireplace would be about here…and that would put your chair right…about…here."

And then he qualified his answer. "Of course we're actually standing in the basement. The chair would be about eight feet above us."

So I asked, "Got a ladder in the truck?"

He did. He brought it out and placed it roughly on the spot where the chair would be. I made my perch eight feet up and took a look. After a few maneuvers, we had angled the ladder to focus the chair on the virgin state land across the lake. The chair would allow a centered view through our "Land of Sky Blue Waters" picture window out onto the deep, cool waters and its loons and otter and surface feeding bass and blue gills that beckon a fisherman and his children.

In the center of the still life that would be our cabin window stood one young white pine tree.

We spiked the spot. And thus our cabin was built around the view from the chair.

Now it is 10 years later. Ten years of growing children, building a business, losing family and loved ones, and finding solace and peace at our days at the cabin.

For the last 10 years, in the view from the chair, I have watched the one young white pine make its way up into view in our window. At first it barely was in frame.

But it kept reaching up.

This year it has finally made its way to the top of the window's vantage, its middle bows now offering a wonderful foreground for our view of the water.

White pines grow slowly, but they become the giants of the north woods. Upon maturity they tower over the other trees. I have come to view the white pine in the window as something of a pet. I pruned its lower branches. Cleared some scrub maple from its reach, and pounded a few fertilizer spikes around its base for good measure. To my eye the tree looks perfect.

In much the same way the pencil marks on our garage door measure the growth of our three children, the white pine in the cabin window, when viewed from the chair, has become something of a measuring stick on the days and the parts of our life that have passed since we built our hiding place.

Our kids, so young when we first came here, are all young adults. I now need spectacles to read books in the chair. Splitting the wood that burns in the fireplace next to the chair requires a few Advil upon completion.

And through it all the white pine has just kept growing.

This November there was an early, heavy wet snow…so heavy that it managed to drop one tree on my car parked in the cabin drive. That snow also took the tops off a lot of the trees along our shoreline, so that now they have a stunted look.

But the white pine in the window managed to shuck off the weight of the snow. It still looks perfect. While interns, wars and plummeting markets grabbed at our attention over the last 10 years, the tree in the window just kept growing. Perfectly.

These are the things you think about.

At the cabin, on the lake, in August. In the chair.

August 2002

FUNNIER THAN A BONE SCAN

Chicago Mike called earlier this week. He has been a friend for several decades, since my early days in Chicago broadcasting.

Pittsburgh born, he is funny, tough and sweet in equal measure. Correction. He is more funny than he is tough or sweet.

After all, it is Mike, a charter member of our annual January ice fishing trip in the wilds of Minocqua, who uttered the following words through an icy face mask on the coldest day of the last century, while we peered numbly at an augured hole in the frigid ice: "If I die first, you guys have permission to eat me to stay alive."

Mike called last week to tell me that he might not be able to join us in that common middle-aged occurrence, a charity golf event.

"You guys may have to find a fourth. They say I need surgery. Looks like I have prostate cancer."

Though stunned, I expressed my concern and optimism. I asked how the family was taking the news.

Mike paused and then said, "Well, my brother didn't say anything for a second… and then he asked if he could have my golf clubs."

The calls to the other ice fishing buddies flew back and forth, expressing concern for Mike's condition, while at the same time searching for the best joke about the diagnosis.

I told Chicago Ron, a screenwriter and director, that I had called another ice fishing buddy, Chicago Larry, a high-powered broadcast exec and amateur hypochondriac. (We call him a hypochondriac because he always eats his salad when we go out for steak.)

I told Ron that when I relayed the distressing news to Larry, I had a sneaking suspicion that Larry immediately began examining his own prostate while we were still on the phone, and that I found that deeply disturbing.

I also told Ron that I had Googled Mike's condition and that the prognosis seemed positive.

Ron paused for a moment and then suggested that I also call Larry so he could stop examining himself at his desk.

A few days later, I called Mike again to see how he was doing. He mentioned that one side effect of the cancer procedure is decreased sexual function. I told him the Billy Wilder joke about the old man who goes to his doctor and complains that he can't pee. The doctor asks the man how old he is. He replies, "Ninety four." The doctor says, "You've peed enough."

Mike laughs. I ask him how his wife is handling that sobering information about those sexual side effects of prostate surgery. Without missing a beat, Mike tells me she sent the urologist a dozen roses.

I ask Mike how everyone was taking the news. He said all the ice fishing guys were helping him goof on the whole thing, but that one of our other hypochondriac buddies was taking things too seriously.

He claimed he had to go to his doctor to have his gland checked because after he got the news, he went to a rock concert and the music was so loud it made his prostate hurt. He left after four songs. And then Mike added, "And it was only a Hall and Oates reunion tour." He waits another moment and then adds, "Unplugged."

We both laugh and talk about this year's ice fishing plans in January.

Then Mike has to ring off.

He has an appointment to get a bone scan.

October 2002

2003

LIKE A ROLLING STONE

This is an important month in my life. Fifty years ago, on a cold February morning, I was born. Soon, very soon, I will be a half-century old.

I hesitate to write a piece about turning 50 because it really isn't that big of a deal. I feel no different. I look the same as I did last week, when I was young and in my 40s.

In fact I have been saying to friends that, thanks to new drugs, healthier living and occasional exercise, 50 today is what 40 was a generation ago.

How's that for denial?

But we keep track of birthdays so that we can keep track of ourselves. Fifty years on the blue ball requires some observation, especially when you write a monthly column that entails offering observations. But I balk at scratching pithy perspective on how people should live just because I have managed to compile 50 years.

Hell, the only reason I am here is because someone invented penicillin.

Sure, I could write something quaint about the fact that there were still veterans of the Civil War who were alive when I was born. Or that I remember television being novel. I could sadden you with memories of JFK's, RFK's or MLK's assassinations. Or make you smile with the excitement of the Beatles shaking their bowl cuts on Ed Sullivan.

But instead I would like to describe to you my set list.

A set list is the order of songs that a rock 'n' roll band sings at a gig. To celebrate my 50th year of life, I would like to take over the Gridiron bar, formerly the Copper Grid and the site of my first legal beer. I would hire the best local session musicians I could find, slurp one Miller Lite for courage while the audience is brought to focus as the house lights dim. With its killer groove I would play Marvin Gaye's live version of the national anthem as sung at an NBA All-Star game in the mid '80s. No better rendition ever.

Then I would ascend the steps to sing a few songs to celebrate the accomplishment of not dying for a half century.

Hell, if Sinatra could look back on when he was 17, so can I at 50.

First, with just a blues harp and piano accompanist, I would warble the ballad version of Bruce Springsteen's *Thunder Road*, beginning with those wonderful words, "The screen door slams, Mary's dress waves. Like a vision she dances across the porch as the radio plays."

From there, a build with my brother Jim, and friend and business partner, Dave Fleer, joining me on stage with their guitars as well as the rest of The Best Band 500 Bucks Can Buy. With layered harmonies and fuller instrumentation, we would play the Beatles classic, *In My Life*.

"There are places I remember..." Great song, Good Beatles harmonies with Davey and Jim.

Then we get moving. Cue the drums. Cue the sax player. Launch into David Bowie's unforgettable *Young Americans*. Tough song to do, but what a great track. Hard to memorize all those lyrics when you are young. Even harder at 50. Need female backup singers, too.

Keep up the tempo with a salute to our favorite locals of years gone by with the Cheap Trick anthem, Surrender. "Mommy's all right. Daddy's all right. They just get a little weird."

Then a Van Morrison number. Perhaps *Brown-Eyed Girl*, a reminder of my wife and daughters. Or *Crazy Love*. Or *Radio*. Or any Van Morrison song at all, with the caveat that no one can sing a Van Morrison song at all well, except for Mr. Morrison.

Then a few dedications.

First a song for my parents. Something Irish. Too early in the night for *Danny Boy*. Make it *Galway Bay*.

Then a song for my kids, Bob Dylan's electric version of *Forever Young*. There is a great cut that he sings with Springsteen. Swing the spotlight into the crowd to find the kids with the words, "May your hand be always steady. May your feet always be swift. May you have a strong foundation as the winds of changes shift."

Then a ballad for the bride. Our latest theme song, *Harvest Moon*. "I want to see you dance again…on this harvest moon."

Not sure what the closing song would be. Always fond of the harmonies of Dream Academy's *Life in a Northern Town*. "In the winter of '63, it felt like the earth would freeze. With John F. Kennedy and the Beatles…take it easy on yourself."

Then I would slip off the stage. Let the real musicians take over. Sit at a table; sip a beer in the dark.

And smile.

February 2003